Scientists as Theologians

Also by John Polkinghorne and published by SPCK:

One World (1986)
Science and Creation (1988)
Science and Providence (1989)
Reason and Reality (1991)
Science and Christian Belief (1994)

Published by Triangle:
The Way the World Is (rev. edn 1992)
Quarks, Chaos and Christianity (1994)

SCIENTISTS AS THEOLOGIANS

A Comparison of the Writings of Ian Barbour, Arthur Peacocke and John Polkinghorne

JOHN POLKINGHORNE

First published in Great Britain 1996
SPCK
Holy Trinity Church
Marylebone Road
London NW1 4DU

British Library Cataloguing in Publication Data
A catalogue record for this book is available from the British Library

ISBN 0-281-04945-9

Typeset by Wilmaset Ltd, Birkenhead, Wirral
Printed in Great Britain by
The Cromwell Press, Melksham, Wiltshire

To
my fellow members
of the Society
of Ordained Scientists

Contents

Preface

CONTRARY TO THE popular but inaccurate picture of science and theology being at loggerheads with each other, the fact of the matter is that there is a lively debate between the two disciplines, and many of the contributors to that debate are themselves scientists with a personal commitment to religion and a serious concern with theology. Three of these scientist-theologians have written quite extensively on these matters, and it is their thought that this book surveys. The writers selected are Ian Barbour, Arthur Peacocke and myself. In making that choice I have excluded scientists who have an interest in a theistic view of the world, but who do not align themselves with any religious tradition (such as Paul Davies) and theologians who pay some attention to science in their writings (such as Philip Hefner, Jürgen Moltmann, Nancey Murphy, Wolfhart Pannenberg, Ted Peters and Thomas Torrance). Narrowing the focus will, I hope, provide greater clarity of vision. There is sufficient common ground and sufficient distinctiveness of view among the scientist-theologians for it to seem worthwhile to survey their contribution to the science and theology debate, albeit from the standpoint of one of those involved.

The three of us so chosen display many common attitudes and understandings, but we also manifest distinct differences of style and strategy. In particular, we make different assessments of the degree to which science and theology can share a common conceptual structure and the degree to which they must insist on the conceptual novelty of their own understanding, while still seeking a consistent account of the truth about reality to which each contributes. At issue is the balance it is possible to achieve between, on the one hand, the necessity for science and theology each to conduct its discourse in the manner proper to its own intellectual needs and, on the other hand, the desire to integrate the two discourses into a single account of the unity of knowledge. Is consonance between the two disciplines sufficient, or should we search for a greater degree of assimilation of each to the other? Similar questions arise within natural science itself, where the different disciplines of physics, chemistry and biology each contribute to an understanding of the physical world in their distinctive ways. Again, there are differing assessments of the appropriate form of their mutual relationships.

Comparing these writers' insights and contributions is clearly rather a delicate task for one who is himself part of the triumvirate. It would be inconsistent for me not to suppose that, when we disagree, the better part of the argument lies with the stance that I have myself espoused. I cannot avoid writing from my own perspective, but I have tried to read my colleagues' valuable work with care and attention and to summarize their insights fairly. I gladly acknowledge how much I have learned over the years from both of them, including the cases where we disagree as well as those where we concur.

In the attempt to be as even-handed as it is possible for an interested party to be, it has seemed important to base the discussion on the published works of the authors, and to allow each to speak in his own words about his own concerns and insights. In consequence, this book includes an unusually large degree of direct quotation. I realize that this may well be a matter of irritation for some readers, but it has seemed necessary in a comparative study of this kind. Some may find it even more regrettable that there is a substantial amount of self-quotation among the citations used. I have felt this to be necessary, rather than resorting always to paraphrase, so that I should be seen to be as accountable for my published opinions as I require my colleagues to be for theirs.

Ian Barbour and Arthur Peacocke were kind enough to read and comment on an early draft of the manuscript. Their remarks have helped me to improve the text significantly, and I am most grateful to them. However, the responsibility for what is written in this book is, of course, mine alone. I know that they will not agree with all that I say.

A book of this kind might hope to achieve two ends. One is to present an overview of the scientist-theologians' contribution to the debate in a way that delineates the shape of the wood for those already familiar with some of the trees. The other is to encourage those readers who have not yet done so, to go on to read some of the books on which this volume is based. Inevitably, I can only here sketch the arguments presented by Barbour, Peacocke and myself. I hope that they will be found sufficiently interesting to encourage further detailed engagement with them.

God is neither male nor female, but I follow the traditional convention by using the pronoun 'he' where necessary.

My secretary, Mrs Josephine Brown, has shown all her customary patience and skill in coping with my handwriting and typing the drafts of the manuscript. I am most grateful to her, as I am to my wife, Ruth, for help in correcting the proofs and to staff of SPCK in preparing this book for publication.

John Polkinghorne
The President's Lodge
Queens' College
Cambridge

ABBREVIATIONS

CWS	A.R. Peacocke: *Creation and the World of Science*
GNB	A.R. Peacocke: *God and the New Biology*
IR	A.R. Peacocke: *Intimations of Reality*
MMP	I.G. Barbour: *Myths, Models and Paradigms*
OW	J.C. Polkinghorne: *One World*
RAS	I.G. Barbour: *Religion in an Age of Science*
RR	J.C. Polkinghorne: *Reason and Reality*
SC	J.C. Polkinghorne: *Science and Creation*
SCB	J.C. Polkinghorne: *Science and Christian Belief*
SP	J.C. Polkinghorne: *Science and Providence*
TSA	A.R. Peacocke: *Theology for a Scientific Age*

I

Introduction

THE ARTICULATION OF theological thought has always been influenced by the prevailing culture. Although theology's subject is divine reality, its discourse is human discourse and no one can escape being influenced by contemporary patterns of thought, with all the opportunities and limitations that that implies. Moreover, those who seek to speak of God are attempting to refer to the One who is the creative ground of all that is. They must, therefore, take into account all that we have learned about the variety of the world. This requires engagement with the full range of human disciplines – from natural science to anthropology and sociology, to aesthetics and ethics – that seek to explore the many-layered reality of our experience. Theology is the great integrative discipline; it is metaphysics practised in the presence of God. Its paradox is that it strives to speak of the Infinite and Eternal while using finite and time-bound human language.

It is easy to illustrate this interaction of theology with culture. St Augustine, whose writings have played so formative a role in the thinking of the Western Church, was deeply influenced by the neoplatonism of his time. In the later Middle Ages, St Thomas Aquinas employed the rediscovered insights of Aristotle in framing the great systematic accounts of the *Summa Theologiae* and the *Summa Contra Gentiles*. Yet neither of these great thinkers was simply adding a pious Christian gloss to secular philosophy. Both used and transformed what culture had made available to them. When Augustine read the prologue to St John's Gospel (John 1.1–14), he found much that was already familiar to him as it spoke of the divine Word, the active principle of order behind the workings of the universe. Yet when he came to the verse 'And the Word became flesh and dwelt among us', he encountered something specifically Christian for which his neoplatonism had not prepared him.

Aquinas' concept of God, however invulnerable that God may seem in his impassibility, is far from the God of Aristotle, totally absorbed in contemplating his own perfection.[1]

Two currents of thought characterize the culture of our own time. One springs from more than a century's engagement with the masters of suspicion, starting with thinkers like Marx and Freud who claimed to reveal that human thought has its origin not in the ostensible objects of its engagement, but in the hidden motivations of class or sex. The collection of contemporary attitudes loosely gathered together under the rubric of 'postmodernism' encourages the assertion of the human construction of our pictures of reality, the affirmation that they derive their meaning not from conformity with the way things are, but from conformity with the way our particular linguistic and cultural community has chosen to speak about them. The text means whatever the reader chooses as response. You have your views; I have mine. Relativism rules.

The second current of thought flows counter to the first. Its spring is the success of modern science in its account of the nature and history of the physical world. Here we seem to see the growth of actual knowledge about the way things are. At least, that is how the scientists themselves see it, though there are many philosophers of science who would offer a more deconstructive account of scientific achievement. They would deny that science is concerned with discovery. Instead, for them, it is also a human construction, arising from a tacit agreement to see things in a particular way. Such critics would admit that science gets things done, but they believe this is only because it employs pragmatically useful manners of speaking, rather than its knowing what things are actually like. The realists counter by asking how this wonderfully effective power could arise, other than from a knowledge of what is actually the case?[2]

Theology is buffeted by both these currents. Religion is concerned with discerning whether there is a divine will giving meaning and purpose to what is happening. If all meaning is a personal human construct, then God can be no more than a self-selected symbol for our individual highest ideals. Religion might be true for me or true for you, as a technique for living, but it could not be just true, pure and simple. In resisting relativism, science and religion can make common cause, but then a perplexing difference arises between them when we consider their relative degrees of success in achieving agreed understanding. One does not have to take a simplistic Whig view of scientific history (as if it were all a tale of majestic and inevitable advance to incontestable success) in order to recognize that the subject makes permanent gains in knowledge. Who can doubt that matter has an atomistic constitution, or that the helically structured DNA molecule is the carrier of genetic information? We have learned some things about the physical world that will not have to be unlearned. Of course, it may well be that they will be modified in detail and in depth. Science constructs maps of the physical world that are accurate for many purposes, but not for *every* purpose. That is why those of us who defend scientific realism must speak in terms of verisimilitude and not in terms of absolute and final truth. Nevertheless, the advance of science is impressive and it contrasts with the endless debates about religion, from which there never seems to issue a universally agreed conclusion. Small wonder, then, that many who wish to rescue science from its postmodernist detractors have often felt willing to leave religion in their deconstructive clutches. This can lead to scientism: the belief that science is the only worthwhile source of knowledge and that it is of itself enough.

It is hard to exaggerate the implausible poverty of a scientistic view of reality.[3] The fact is that science has purchased its success by the modesty of its exploratory and explanatory ambitions. It limits itself to an impersonal encounter with the world, deliberately bracketing out those personal experiences that give human life its greatest satisfactions. I believe that such a desiccated account of things cannot even accommodate the practice of science itself, which requires unspecifiable acts of judgement, assessed within a truth-seeking community, and whose chief reward is the experience of wonder at the rational beauty and fruitfulness of the universe.[4] Langdon Gilkey rightly says, 'Not all that we know is science, lest there be no possibility of science.'[5]

Accordingly, there have been a number of writers who have adopted a strategy of aligning theology and science in a common struggle against a twentieth-century despair of any knowledge of reality.[6] Methodologically they discern a concern, shared between the two disciplines, with the search for motivated belief arising from encounter with the presence of creation and its Creator. They believe that it is possible to attain best explanations of experience that correspond to a verisimilitudinous account of what is going on. They acknowledge that there are constraints of cultural perspective and expectation to be taken into account in assessing this search for understanding, but they believe these constraints can be allowed for and that they do not determine the outcome of the inquiry. The latter arises from conformity with the way things are. Such a stance is usually called 'critical realism'. Its adherents explain the differences between the two disciplines in achieving agreed conclusions, with reference to science's being able to deal with a physical world that we transcend and that we can put to the experimental test, while theology is concerned with God, who transcends us and veils his infinite reality from direct contact with our finite being.

Those who adopt this position must then go on to ask what is the relationship between the contents of knowledge proffered by natural science on the one hand and theology on the other. If it is the one world of existing reality that both are investigating, then the stories they tell of it must be reconcilable with each other. Pursuit of this question has been the special concern of those I have called the scientist-theologians: people whose initial academic experience has been in some branch of natural science, but whose Christian faith has moved them to engage also with theological questions. The writings of three such authors are the main concern of this book: Ian Barbour,[7] Arthur Peacocke[8] and myself.[9] I wish both to indicate the substantial areas of agreement between us and also to identify and discuss the matters of disagreement that begin to emerge as the development of the science and theology debate moves its participants into closer engagement with central questions of Christian theology.

Ian Barbour[10] has given a helpful fourfold taxonomy of possible ways of relating science and religion. (I would prefer in fact to say 'science and theology', since it is the intellectual reflection on religion that closely parallels science's intellectual reflection on the physical world.) His categories are: conflict; independence; dialogue; integration.

Conflict occurs when either discipline attempts to assert control over the rightful domain of inquiry of the other. We have already noticed this happening in scientism's claim that the only questions worth asking, and capable of being answered, are those that lie within the competency of science itself. An analogous takeover bid from the side of religion would be a creationist claim that a literal interpretation of biblical writings determines the agenda for understanding the process and history of the universe. The implausibility of such narrow dogmatisms scarcely needs elaboration.

At first sight, the assertion of independence appears more plausible. Do not science and religion refer to different realms of experience (the impersonal, and the personal) and ask different questions (How do things happen? Why are things happening?)? If this were all that could be said, then the two subjects would be separate, each insulated from impact with the other. Agnostic scientists are often happy to agree a truce with religion on these terms. Yet a little reflection shows that independence is too simplistic a description. 'How?' and 'Why?' may be different questions, but their respective answers must bear some consistent relationship to each other. The discovery that the universe has had a long evolutionary history, and that it did not come into being recently and ready-made, has certainly caused theologians to think in new ways about how to understand their fundamental assertion of the Creator's will lying behind what is happening.

Dialogue recognizes that science and religion have things to say to each other. My own characterization of that mutual conversation would be that religion must listen to what science has to tell it about the nature and history of the physical world, and that religion can offer science a deeper and more comprehensive account of reality within which the latter's search for understanding can find an intellectually comfortable home.[11]

Integration would seem to imply a still closer relationship. Barbour's examples include the current revival of natural theology[12] and various attempts at a theology of nature.[13] In the main, these seem to me to be examples of dialogue, in which there is insightful exchange without pretence of a necessary fusion between the two subjects, though Teilhard de Chardin certainly seems to be an integrationist. Still more integrative in intention is Barbour's third example of the use of A. N. Whitehead's process philosophy to provide a common metaphysical basis for understanding both science and religion. I shall be commenting on the programme of process theology as the discussion develops.

As one would expect, the scientist-theologians reject the way of conflict; the extremes of scientism and creationism hold no attractions for them. Equally, they decline to espouse the thesis of two independent languages, for they find that science and religion in fact have important things to say to each other. Our common ground is, therefore, in the area of dialogue-integration, but we strike the balance between scientific and theological considerations in somewhat different ways. I would prefer to redescribe this territory in order to make the differences in attitude, as I see them, more evident.

My own classification of possible forms of an interactive relationship between science and religion is also twofold. The viable options are:

(a) *Consonance.*[14] Science does not determine theological thought but it certainly constrains it. Physics provides the ground plan for the edifice of metaphysics. The form of the latter is not entailed, but its shape is certainly restricted by the discoveries of science. The scientific and theological accounts of the world must fit together in a mutually consistent way. In fact, because I also accept the dialogue description of this relationship, I believe that they can do so – not as a mere matter of compatibility, but with a degree of mutual enhancement and enlightenment. The search for consonance is the basis of my own approach to the question of interrelationship. We shall see that it faces one of its most acute challenges when concern centres on questions of how we may conceive of God's action in the world. It is a sign of the deepening seriousness of the encounter of science with theology that the matter of divine agency is a central topic of current discussion.[15] My search for consonance encourages me to a certain boldness in speculating what might be the 'causal joint' of providential interaction.

(b) *Assimilation*. Here, the attempt is made to achieve a greater degree of merging of the two disciplines. What is involved is far from a total absorption of one discipline by the other, but there is a degree of accommodation of the one to the other that could seem to threaten the former's justified autonomy. In practice, given the manifest power of science in its rightful domain, this stance will always carry the danger of the subordination of the theological to the scientific. It is theology that will tend to be assimilated into science.

It is clear from reading reviews of books about science and theology that many people are hoping for a degree of conceptual unification that, in my view, fails to respect the due degree of autonomy that each pattern of inquiry must maintain if it is to be true to itself. Each has its own particular subject matter and its own resulting conceptual system, which have to be respected and which cannot just be transferred across to the other.[16] Central to Christianity is its according a unique status to Jesus Christ. The theological wrestling with how to describe that significance is the subject matter of Christology. I believe that this calls for theological categories that are as radically novel and surprising as were the physical categories found necessary by science to accommodate the phenomena of quantum physics. Those of an assimilative cast of mind have tended to employ evolutionary notions of Christ as a 'new emergent', which I believe are seriously inadequate to the phenomenon one is attempting to understand.[17] I will have more to say about that later.

Theologians also have fallen into the trap of too easy an

assimilation. They often seem to think that twentieth-century scientific talk about the energetic basis of physical reality is somehow more spiritual than nineteenth-century materialism, oblivious of the fact that Einstein's celebrated equation – $E = mc^2$ – as much asserts the materiality (inertia) of energy as it does the energetic character of matter. Wolfhart Pannenberg[18] seems to think that modern field theory offers a way of thinking about spirit, though to a physicist a field is about as spiritual as a tenuous gas!

In the discussion that follows, I believe that a main source of divergence between myself and Barbour and Peacocke will be found to lie in the degree to which one needs to pursue an assimilative strategy and the degree to which one can press the search for specific areas of consonance. When the central topics of the science and theology debate were insights relating to natural theology (the rational intelligibility and finely tuned fruitfulness of the cosmos perceived as rumours of divinity), or continuing creation (the contingencies of evolutionary history perceived as free explorations of fertile possibility), or the combating of a crass reductionism (emerging novelty makes the whole more than the sum of its parts), then considerable unanimity could be found among its Christian participants. As the discussion has moved on from the periphery of contact between science and theology and come closer to the heart of the latter's concerns, divergencies have begun to appear between us.

It is significant that all three of us have recently produced books that might be called mini-systematic theologies,[19] attempting to grapple with the range of Christian belief approached from the viewpoint of a scientist-theologian. Barbour's book is the one least obviously organized in this way, but its sections include discussions of the biblical view of human nature, the role of Christ, God's action in the world, and the problem of evil and suffering. It is characteristic of Barbour's method that he prefaces each discussion with a careful and fair-minded survey of the views of others, but his conclusions are framed in terms of a revised process-theological account, and his book can be read as the approach to Christian theology by one who is seeking to strike a judicious balance between the insights of Whitehead and the insights of modern science, while also taking account of general insights derived from the Bible and Christian experience.

Peacocke's book (in its enlarged form) is more overtly systematic, with a sustained theme being the recognition that we live in a dynamic world of becoming, and not in a static world of being. He is concerned with God as interacting with creation, influencing patterns of events in it, including those in human life and experience.

My own book was deliberately largely woven round phrases selected from the Nicene Creed. Its approach sought to be that of a 'bottom-up thinker' – that is to say, someone who tries to move from the particularities of experience to the generalities of understanding, in the search for motivated belief. I acknowledged then that 'my aim is not to survey the scene but to propose an interpretation'.[20] The time has now come for a broader engagement with the issues.

Having put my own point of view, and being conscious of some divergencies from my respected colleagues, I feel that it would be helpful to attempt a wider and more comparative discussion. It has seemed possible to identify certain general concerns that are to be found in the writings of late twentieth-century scientist-theologians. All wish to see understanding in both science and religion treated as arising from motivated belief, hence our concern with critical realism. All understand human beings as psychosomatic unities, and so we seek to understand human agency and, by analogy, divine agency, as accommodated within some flexible account of physical process. All take with utmost seriousness what science can tell us about the 15-billion-year history of the universe and its rationally beautiful physical fabric. Our discussions of the doctrine of creation and of the possibility of a revived and revised natural theology can only be founded on that basis. All are conscious of the variety, stability and different understandings of the great world faith traditions. Our thinking must seek some ecumenical embrace of this perplexing diversity. All of us, nevertheless, take our stand within the Christian tradition. Each has to articulate how he understands the particularities of Christian belief.

These topics provide a loose framework within which much of the contemporary science and theology debate is being conducted. The chapters that follow will take these general features and see how they are addressed by different participants in the debate.

2

Motivated Belief: Critical Realism

IF THE SCIENCE and theology debate is to take place in a realistic fashion that does justice to both disciplines, then it has to proceed on the basis of certain agreements about how it is to be conducted. I have already emphasized that both science and theology are to be taken seriously as rational endeavours to understand the reality of our experience, a view I share with my scientist-theologian colleagues. We need a willingness to recognize the many-layered character of that experience, so that the same event can be interpreted as a part of physical process, as an occasion for moral decision, as the carrier of beauty, and as an encounter with the divine presence. A crass physical reductionism will exclude by decree not only religion, but also the truly humane. All the writers we are considering agree in seeing their task as concerned with the construction of a comprehensive and unified view of reality, within which both theology and science are contained and are able to interact with each other. Opposing the notion that science and theology are totally separate from each other, Barbour writes that 'We cannot remain content with a plurality of languages if they are languages about the same world. If we seek a coherent interpretation of all experience, we cannot avoid the search for a unified world view.'[1] For his part, Peacocke declares:

> There is a hierarchy of order in the natural world, and, if God is the reality that Christians believe he is, the ways of science and of Christian faith must always, in my view, be ultimately converging. I cannot but see, in the light of this, the scientific and theological enterprises as interacting and mutually illuminating approaches to reality.[2]

My own view is that theology has a dual role. As systematic theology, it is a particular discipline, concerned with those aspects of our encounter with reality that serve as the specific vehicles of religious experience. As philosophical theology, it is seeking to act as the great integrating discipline that expresses the unity of our knowledge of the one world of our experience. Those who endeavour to speak of God as the ground of all, must seek to incorporate all forms of specific knowledge into a single reconciled account. 'Because I regard the existence of God as the ground for the possibility of this latter integrating discipline, I prefer to call it philosophical theology rather than metaphysics.'[3] Without such a ground of unity, the many-layered structure of our experience is hard to comprehend:

> For the theist, the rational beauty of the physical world is not just brute fact, but a reflection of the mind of the Creator. Aesthetic experience and ethical intuitions are not just psychological or social constructs but intimations of God's joy in creation and of his just will. Religious experience is not illusory human projection, but encounter with divine reality. There is an integrating wholeness in the theistic account which I find intellectually satisfying, even though it must wrestle with the mystery of infinite Being.[4]

All three authors agree that science and theology are indispensable partners, together with other forms of human inquiry such as aesthetics and ethics, in the even-handed evaluation of all levels of the exploration of reality and in the search for a unified account of resulting human knowledge. This point is frequently at issue in dialogue with unbelieving scientists. The latter often espouse a covert scientism that attributes subjective experiences of beauty and moral imperative to the contingent 'hard wiring' of the human brain, developed to implement a portfolio of evolutionary strategies for survival. The humane is reduced to the merely epiphenomenal. I have attempted elsewhere to exhibit the implausibility of this reduction.[5] It is a stance that accords ill with the seriousness with which many scientists enjoy and value the beauty of music. The latter is certainly more than vibrations in the air.

Another important point in common to all three authors is that we write from within the worshipping life of the community of the Church. Revelation is understood in terms of the human encounter with divine grace, and not as the uncritical acceptance of some unquestionable propositional knowledge made known by an infallible decree. It is *data*, not divinely dictated theory. Barbour says, 'The context of theology is always the worshipping community',[6] and concerning revelation he writes:

> Special events in the past enable us to see what is present at other times but may have been ignored. The cross reveals God's universal love, everywhere expressed but not everywhere acknowledged ... [Revelation] is not a system of divine propositions completed in the past but an invitation to new experience of God today.[7]

Concerning a belief in divine providence, Peacocke writes that it 'is founded existentially on Christian experience, indeed on religious experience in general, and forms the presupposition of prayer, worship and the daily lives of believers'.[8] His concluding chapter is woven round the means of grace: 'They include the Bible, prayer, worship and the sacraments.'[9] For my own part, I have related 'the universe-assisted logic' of science (which needs the experimental nudge of nature in the formation of its theories) to the 'liturgy-assisted logic' of theology (which finds its inspiration in the experience of worship, particularly the Eucharist).[10] Elsewhere I have written, 'Worship and prayer is the context in which theology has to be practised: the academic departments of religious studies in our universities are like schools of science unfurnished with laboratories.'[11] A similar view has also been taken by Nancey Murphy, who points to an interesting contrast arising from the difference between widespread participation in the common Christian life and the specially contrived experience created in the scientific laboratory: 'In physics, nearly all knowledge comes from the professional to the amateur. In the case of theology, as here envisioned, knowledge of God begins with the amateurs ... and the professional theologian is dependent on the findings of this community.'[12]

The rooting of knowledge in interpreted experience treated as a reliable guide to the nature of reality is an intellectual commitment that we may call 'realism'. Motivated belief is held to afford an insight into what is actually the case. The scientist-theologians all adopt such a stance in relation both to science and to theology, and regard it as the basis for a cousinly comradeship between the two disciplines.[13] Each has his own way of encapsulating the realist attitude. I have coined the slogan 'Epistemology models Ontology': in other words, what we know is a reliable guide to what is the case. Barbour says that, 'The basic assumption of realism is that *existence* is prior to *theorizing*'[14] – that is, it is encounter with the actually existing nature of the world that prompts our thoughts about it. Peacocke remarks, 'In practice, working scientists, I would argue, adopt a sceptical and qualified realism, according to which their theories and models are proposed and regarded as "candidates for reality".'[15]

This last remark reminds us that it is a *critical* realism that the scientist-theologians defend. No naïve objectivity is involved in either discipline; both science and theology speak of entities not directly observable by us. The quarks and gluons, which are believed to be the fundamental constituents of nuclear matter, are also thought to be confined – that is to say, so tightly bound within the particles that they constitute, that they will never be observable separately in isolation. Their existence is inferred from the way in which its assumption makes sense of great swathes of physical data.[16] God is not available for direct inspection. His unseen presence is inferred from the way that this makes sense of great swathes of spiritual experience. I have added to my critical realism the suggestion that it is intelligibility that is the key to reality,[17] an attitude I first adopted in the course of seeking to defend the reality of the elusive and unpicturable quantum world.[18] Entities with explanatory power are candidates for acceptance as components of reality. What makes sense of extensive experience is to be treated with ontological seriousness. Here is a particular way of expressing the realist conviction so natural to a scientist and so necessary for a theologian.

Intelligibility requires the adoption of a prior interpretative point of view in the effort to make sense of what is going on. Another reason why our realism must be qualified as 'critical' lies in this need to don these theoretical spectacles in the attempt to perceive pattern in the flux of events. Neither in science nor in theology will we derive much insight from simply staring at raw data. The chosen initial point of view must be open to correction in the light of further experience, but it cannot be dispensed with and this introduces an element of circularity into the quest for understanding.[19] There is both a hermeneutic circularity (we must adopt a point of view in order to understand experience; experience must confirm or modify our chosen point of view) and an epistemic circularity (how we know is controlled by the nature of the object of our knowledge; and that nature is revealed through our knowledge of the object). This latter point is of great importance for the science and theology debate. Scientists too often assume that there is a universal epistemology, which they then, of course, equate with that of their own particular discipline. Even within science itself this Procrustean approach is clearly unsatisfactory. Ethology and elementary particle physics gain knowledge of the objects of their study in entirely different ways. In the domain of our humane encounter with each other, with moral duty and aesthetic delight, with the awesome and hopeful reality of God, ways of knowing are involved that are ineluctably personal and that cannot be reduced to the impersonal protocol appropriate to a scientific experiment. We have once again returned to the fundamental matter of the many-layered character of human experience. The different layers are encountered and known in their own appropriate ways.

Circularity clearly introduces an element of precariousness into our intellectual endeavour. What if our understanding were to prove no more than a self-supporting house of cards, a confection condemned to immediate collapse once one of its arbitrary components is removed? A realist must have a reply to this critique, and mine would involve two observations.

The first is that I do not think we have any choice, either in science or theology, about adopting a strategy that calls for careful acts of intellectual daring. We have to stick our necks out if we are to be able to see anything. The Cartesian and Enlightenment programme of the search for clear and certain ideas as the basis for unshakeable knowledge has simply proved to be a failure. It would have been nice if it could have succeeded, but we have discovered painfully that it has not. I am sufficiently postmodern to recognize that this is the case.

This acknowledgement, however, does not lead me to intellectual despair, for my second observation is that our minds are so constituted, and we live in a world itself so constituted, that intellectual daring in the pursuit of a strategy of cautious circularity proves capable of yielding reliable knowledge. I say that not because the world *had* to be that way, but because, as a matter of contingent fact, it has proved to be so. The defence of critical realism depends upon an appeal to historical experience rather than to metaphysical necessity. We do appear able to gain knowledge of what is the case.

That seems most clear in relation to the success of science.[20] Of course, there are changes in our detailed understanding of the entities about which physical science seeks to speak. J. J. Thompson, the discoverer of the electron, thought about these tiny electrically charged particles in one way, Niels Bohr in another, Paul Dirac in another, and Feynman, Schwinger and Tomonaga (the discoverers of modern quantum electrodynamics) in yet another. Yet it is perfectly natural to say that they were all describing the same entity and that the difference in their discourse relates to a deepening of our understanding of the nature of electrons. There are continuities in what is being said (all are talking about a particle with mass of about 10^{-27}gm and with a certain electric charge, a constituent of atoms), and one can see how the classical account of Thompson is a crude approximation to the increasingly more subtle quantum mechanical descriptions of his successors. What is happening is not discontinuous change, but better understanding. A critical realist cannot claim the attainment of absolute truth, but rather an increasing verisimilitude – the construction of better and better maps of physical reality.

In evaluating this historical assertion, it must be borne in mind that the advance of twentieth-century science has been so rapid that there are several generations of scientific change over which to assess the claim of a tightening grasp of an actual reality. In elementary particle physics we have moved from lingering doubts about atoms at the start of the century, to the present 'Standard Model' of quarks and gluons, with the discovery of the existence of the nucleus and the elucidations of atomic structure and nuclear structure lying in between. A hundred years has afforded much experience against which to test the critical realist claim.

Clearly, the historical defence of critical realism in theology is a more tricky undertaking. One could not assert that the subject has been characterized by the same power of its community to reach agreed conclusions, which is such an impressive feature of the cumulative advance of science. Yet, to take the Western Christian tradition as an example, one can perceive within the great succession of Augustine, Aquinas, Luther, Calvin, Schleiermacher and Barth a continuing exploration and appropriation of the foundational riches of the New Testament. In the history of holiness, which is part of the history of the Church (despite the presence also of demonic distortion within that history), one can perceive a continuous spiritual engagement with divine reality. Perhaps rather more than my scientist-theologian colleagues, I am anxious to locate our twentieth-century understandings within that development of Christian doctrine, to stress continuity rather than discontinuity with the past, without denying the particular insights available in the present.[21]

The principal difference between science and theology surely lies in the character of the experience that motivates their belief. In experimental science there is always the opportunity for repetition. Again, that is a contingent fact about the world, but one that is so familiar and well established that we seldom pause to think about it. We do not doubt that we have access to the same kind of electrons that J. J. Thompson discovered, or that Willis Lamb investigated in a sensitive experiment that triggered the discovery of modern quantum electrodynamics. Although Peacocke says (in relation to electrons, as it happens) that reference takes place within 'the social chain in a continuous linguistic community',[22] that chain could be broken, and its links subsequently re-established, simply through this universal accessibility to fundamental physical entities. If some great disaster obliterated all human knowledge of electrodynamics, later generations could recapitulate the discoveries and, if subsequently antique scientific records came to light, assure themselves that they were talking about what previous generations had called 'electrons'.

Theology depends for its moments of transparency to the divine upon events and people that are unrepeatably unique. The eternal God has made himself known, in Israel and through Jesus Christ, in occasions of historical particularity. Christianity as such would disappear if all the records and recall of the New Testament and of church history were to be obliterated. In the realm of the personal and the transpersonal, uniqueness by no means implies unreality – quite the reverse in fact, for it is the essence of these regimes that they are concerned with what is individual and not reducible to a uniform and monochrome account. It does mean, however, that access to what motivates theological belief is to be had within a history and within a tradition of practice. We shall return to these issues in a later chapter when we consider the problems posed by the stable existence of diverse faith traditions.

The verisimilitudinous nature of our knowledge in science, and even more so in theology (whose finite discourse will never be adequate to the Infinite Reality of which it purports to speak), means that participants in the science and theology debate have often had recourse to concepts such as models or metaphors to describe the character of their understanding.[23] There are a variety of ways in which such ideas can be put to work, and a variety of shades of meaning that the terms can be made to carry. I find that I differ in some details from the practice of my colleagues in this respect.

I want to make a clear distinction between model and

metaphor. Models are used in science as exploratory devices, useful in the attempt to gain some understanding of a limited aspect of physical phenomena.[24] They abstract those features of the situation that are presumed to be significant in the generation of the particular effects being considered, and they seek to see if the construct thus produced proves indeed to afford insight into what is going on. There is no reason to treat models with ontological seriousness, as if they were approximate maps of reality. They are simply crude pictures of a particular process. For example, there was a version of the quark model of matter that pictured quarks as free to rattle around within the impenetrable walls of a container. This scored some successes in interpreting the energy states of hadronic (i.e. strongly interacting) matter, but no one supposed that hadrons were in fact 'bags' (to give the model its technical name!).

Barbour concurs with this notion of models as exploratory devices when he writes, 'Broadly speaking a model is a symbolic representation of selected aspects of the behaviour of a complex system. It is an imaginative tool for ordering experience, rather than a description of the world.'[25] Peacocke, on the other hand, quotes with apparent approval a much broader definition given by Janet Martin Soskice, stating that 'an object or state of affairs is a model when it is viewed in terms of its resemblance, real or imaginary, to some other object or state of affairs'.[26] The exploratory intention is not brought into focus by this definition.

Models are prosaic devices aiding investigation, useful in the attempt to get some purchase on particular processes. Metaphors are allusive literary devices that illuminate a situation, not by a kind of painstaking partial correspondence with aspects of another situation, but by a disclosure rooted in the unexpected juxtaposition of what is fundamentally dissimilar. Metaphors are poetic revelatory devices, useful in the attempt to probe beneath the surface of appearance. The typical example of a model is the often-analysed case of the kinetic theory of gases, treating tenuous matter as if it were composed of freely moving, perfectly elastic, billiard-ball molecules; the typical example of a metaphor is the often-analysed statement

'Man is wolf', whose content cannot be spelt out in such itemized terms. The difference between model and metaphor is analogous to the difference between the scheme of an allegory and the intuitive insight of a parable.

Science makes frequent use of models. I doubt whether it makes much, if any, use of metaphor. Exciting though science is, its natural discourse is prose and not poetry. I feel some dissent, therefore, when Peacocke says that science 'seeks to provide answers to the question "why?" by depicting the realities of the natural world in metaphorical language'.[27] (I would also prefer to reserve 'why?' as a question relating to theology's concerns with meaning and purpose, and to regard science's concern with physical process as answering the question 'how?'.) Barbour stresses the irreplaceability of metaphor because it is intrinsically open-ended in its application, but he regards models as also possessing this property. In his view, the distinction lies in the systematic character of models and the emotional and valuational overtones carried by metaphor.[28] I wish to resist the assimilation of the distinct categories of metaphor and model to each other. In my opinion, when scientists use apparently metaphorical language – as in talk of 'black holes' or the 'genetic code' – they are using these terms as picturesque shorthand for ideas that they can readily and more adequately convey in precise scientific language, and they are not using them as imaginative resources for the generation of ideas in a truly metaphorical way. Even biologists, who are certainly more given to this way of speaking than physicists, seem to me to be more concerned with the plain comparison of a simile.

Metaphor, in my view, is not intrinsic to scientific discourse, but it certainly is to theological discourse. The latter's need to use finite language about the uncapturable infinity of the divine nature requires the indefinite open-endedness that metaphor affords, its poetic power to grant intuitive illumination. In fact, theology must go beyond the literary device of metaphor and make use of the broader concept of symbol.[29] Symbols exceed signs in their possessing a profound power to participate in that which they represent. They verge on the sacramental and they are an indispensable expression of the life of worship.

This recourse to symbol does not mean that the more prosaic forms of theological discussion do not also make use of models. We are familiar with models of God (loving Father, stern Judge), with models of the atonement (propitiation, satisfaction, victory over the powers), and with the models drawn from the tradition of Israel (Son of God, Wisdom, prophet) that the New Testament writers employ in their search for an adequate manner of speaking about the event of Christ.[30]

The limited scope of any one model's explanatory ambition, and the fact that it is not proposed as an adequate ontological description, means that there is no perplexity about the use of a portfolio of different models, and no necessity to seek their perfect reconciliation with each other. We no more need to resolve the tension between the divine models of God as Father and as Judge than we need to do the same for the physical models of the nucleus as a cloudy crystal ball and as a liquid drop. They simply serve to shed modest light on different, mutually exclusive, aspects of our experience. As Barbour says, we need to take them 'seriously but not literally'.[31]

A scientist will not rest content with a collection of models, however useful they may be when used with discrimination and discretion. Rather, the scientist will want to press on, if possible, to the construction of a theory. The latter I understand to be an account that affords consistent explanation of phenomena over a wide and clearly demarcated range of well-winnowed physical experience, and that is therefore a candidate for the verisimilitudinous description of that domain of the physical world. Theories have serious ontological pretensions, within the acknowledged limits of a critical realism.

Sometimes we possess a theory, but need the help of models in the approximate elucidation of its consequences. No one supposes that the non-relativistic quantum mechanical theory of the electromagnetic interactions of atoms is not the basis of theoretical chemistry, yet working out its consequences is so complex that we often need different models of valency as aids in our search for understanding.

Barbour and Peacocke both believe that models are also aids to the discovery of theories. The former writes, 'One of the functions of models in science is to suggest theories which correlate patterns of observational data',[32] and the latter says, 'Building a scientific theory turns out to be a matter of constructing a proper analogy, and this analogy is provided by a model which is then a source of metaphorical theoretical ideas'.[33] These remarks do not correspond to the way that theories have actually been discovered in fundamental physics. They emerge through a creative insight, often assisted by the search for a relevant formulation endowed with the unmistakable character of mathematical beauty. If fundamental theories owe any debt to previous model-making, it is simply that the models have been part of the engagement with the phenomena that the theory will now be found to explain. Einstein's discovery of general relativity, and Dirac's discovery of the relativistic equation of the electron, had no obligation whatsoever to prior phenomenology, but sprang fully formed from the deep intuition of their originators. Bohr's model of the atom, and the various kinds of quark models, certainly helped in the winnowing of physical phenomena, but the eventual theories of non-relativistic quantum mechanics and quantum chromodynamics, respectively, were strikingly different in kind from their exploratory predecessors. The ability of people of genius to make the imaginative leap to a profound scientific theory is one of the most remarkable properties of the human mind. I would wish to stress its discontinuity, rather than continuity, with the more humdrum activity of model-making.

The differences between Barbour, Peacocke and myself about how it is best to understand and use the concepts of model and metaphor in science are undoubtedly influenced by our differing experiences of doing science. For example, Peacocke was an experimental biochemist; I was a theoretical elementary particle physicist. The kind of ambitious mathematical theories to which fundamental physics successfully aspires cannot be expected to be attained in more complex and subtle subjects such as biochemistry or geophysics. The hexagonal picture of the structure of the benzene ring or the plate tectonics account of continental drift are the form that theories (that is, candidate descriptions of reality) take in these disciplines. I would not call them models, because of their ontological seriousness, nor would I call them metaphors for it is a straightforward comparison that is being invoked in these cases. I find it useful to restrict the term 'model' to cases of acknowledged partial description and limited adequacy. That is also, I believe, how the concept functions in theology.

Theology knows that all its models of God, if pressed too far, will eventually become inadequate idols. It also knows, from the warnings of apophatic theology concerning the unknowable mystery of the divine nature, that its pretensions to theory-making are never going to find adequate fulfilment. However, that does not lead it to intellectual despair, but to cautious modesty about its achievements.[34]

Within the limitations of theological modelling, it may be that certain ideas drawn from science may have a degree of analogical utility. One concept that some have felt worth borrowing is that of complementarity. In quantum physics, we find that certain apparently incompatible descriptions need nevertheless to be used in mutually exclusive circumstances. The quintessential example is the ambiguous wave/particle character of all quantum entities.[35]

In the mind of a Christian, this immediately provokes a comparison with the mixture of divine and human language that traditional Christian discourse has always found to be necessary in speaking of Jesus Christ. Complementarity may be of some value in Christology *if* it is regarded as an encouragement to hold fast to parts of experience whose mutual reconciliation is at first sight extremely difficult to achieve, but *not* if it is regarded as itself being somehow an explanation when one invokes the idea of complementarity outside the physical domain in which it is in fact well understood.[36]

There is a second aspect of quantum complementarity – namely, that it is possible to give two descriptions of physical process; these are of different kinds, but each is in principle complete in itself. (Technically, the simplest example is the configuration space and momentum space formulations of quantum mechanics.) Some writers have suggested this as a helpful analogy to how scientific and religious descriptions of reality might relate to each other. Barbour has resisted this, saying that science and religion, 'arise typically in differing situations and serve differing functions in human life. For this reason I will speak of science and religion as alternative languages, and restrict the term "complementarity" to models of the same logical type *within* a given language'.[37] I think this disjunction is too severe, and I see some value in regarding big bang cosmology and the doctrine of creation as complementary accounts of the coming-to-be of the universe, analogous to the complementarity of acoustical and musicological accounts of a Beethoven quartet.

Theology in an age of science will have to base itself upon the appeal to motivated belief, arising from a critical realist interpretation of its proper domain of religious experience. I entirely agree with Peacocke that:

> For any theology to be believable it will have to satisfy the criteria of reasonableness that lead us to infer the best explanation of the broader features of the natural world ('natural theology' traditionally), and of what men and women believe to be their experiences of 'God'. Truths that are claimed to be revealed or are the promulgations of ecclesiastical authority cannot avoid running the gauntlet of these criteria of reasonableness, for they cannot at the same time be self-warranting and convincing.[38]

The considerations given above encourage the view that there is a critical realist way of doing theology that can meet this challenge. Every generation must seek to sift and make its own, in its own way, the insights handed on to it by Christian Scripture and tradition. However, I become uneasy when Peacocke says, 'even when the traditional words are used in creeds and worship by a twentieth century Christian, the content of their belief bears only a *distant* genetic relationship to what was believed in the context of the thought-world centuries, or even a millennium, ago'.[39]

I wrote my own Gifford lectures 'to explore to what extent we can use the search for motivated understanding, so congenial to the scientific mind, as a route to being able to make the substance of Christian orthodoxy our own' and my conclusion was that one could attain a Christian belief 'which is certainly revised in the light of our twentieth-century insights but which is recognizably contained within an envelope of understanding in continuity with the developing doctrine of the Church through the centuries'.[40]

The point at issue is the extent to which taking science seriously requires us to modify orthodox belief. Will the attainment of consonance between science and theology enable us to fulfil the programme I have defended, or will there be a need for an assimilation of theology to science to an extent that will lead to fundamental modification of the former? How constraining for theological reflection must be the encounter with the insights of twentieth-century science? All three scientist-theologians acknowledge the necessity for, and indeed the value of, some degree of revision, but the discussions that follow will show contrasting assessments of the radicality with which this revision must be undertaken.

3
Embodied Existence: Agency

HUMAN BEINGS ARE inhabitants of the physical world. Twentieth-century theology must take matter seriously, an obligation laid in any case on Christian thought, one of whose central assertions is that 'The Word was made flesh' (John 1.14). This necessity by no means implies that humankind is *merely* material; and Peacocke can speak for all three scientist-theologians in dismissing a crass reductionism by asserting that

> terms such as 'consciousness', 'person', 'social fact' and, in general, the languages of the humanities, ethics, the arts and theology, to name but a few, are not prematurely to be dismissed from the vocabulary used to describe the human condition, since in all these instances a strong case can be made for the distinctiveness and non-reducibility of the concepts they deploy.[1]

In particular, he comments that 'oddly enough, there are signs of a kind of misfit between human beings, persons, and their environment which is not apparent in other creatures'.[2] He instances the act of suicide, and human sadness and protest at mortality. I have said much the same when, after describing some 'signals of transcendence' discerned by Peter Berger,[3] I went on to refer to 'a less focused recognition of unbounded aspiration in the face of human finitude, a stubborn refusal to give the last word to human insignificance on the cosmic scene', which seemed to me to indicate 'that dimension of openness to something beyond us which I have called spiritual, and which carries in the midst of time the hint of eternity'.[4]

The last remark can serve also to remind us that twentieth-century theology must take temporality seriously. In our century, even the universe has been found to have a history, and an understanding of the world in which we live most naturally finds expression in terms of dynamic becoming rather than static being. Heraclitus' proclamation that all is in a state of flux has at last won out over Parmenides' championing of an unchanging reality. Once again, this imposes an obligation not altogether strange to Christianity. The God of the Bible is One who is active in and through the unfolding drama of history.

In fact, there has recently been an increasing engagement in the science and theology debate with the questions and problems of divine action.[5] Because such discussions invariably make some appeal to the analogy to human agency, they raise also issues of human embodied existence. Thus the discussion serves to survey a wide scene.

Topics such as body, mind and spirit, agency, temporality and eternity are the concern of metaphysics; one of the clearest differences between the writers under review relates to their attitude to metaphysical systems.

Barbour[6] has consistently based his thinking on the process metaphysics of A. N. Whitehead.[7] The fundamental metaphysical unit is the event ('an actual occasion'), which has what is called its prehensive phase (the 'survey' of the possibilities of the open future in relation to the events of the past and the divine 'lure' to a certain direction of occurrence), and then its concrescent phase (in which one of these possibilities is actualized). The volitional character of process language, however modified by the liberal application of quotation marks, has led some to criticize what they see as its panpsychism, the unduly wide attribution of mind-like qualities. Barbour regards this as something of a caricature. He writes, 'Whitehead thus does not attribute mind or mentality (as ordinarily understood) to lower-level entities, but he does attribute at least *rudimentary forms of experience* to unified entities at all levels, which runs against the assumptions of many scientists.'[8] Barbour is no fundamentalist process-thinker, for he sees that revisions in Whitehead's scheme are necessary. He thinks that in describing humanity, the episodic character of the process account gives too fleeting a description, which is not adequate to the experience of the continuing identity of the human self. Concerning the inanimate world, he writes:

> The Whiteheadian analysis does not present any direct inconsistency with contemporary science. Creativity is said to be either totally absent (in the case of stones and inanimate objects, which are aggregates without integration or unified experience) or so attenuated that it would escape detection (in the case of atoms). A vanishingly small novelty and self-determination in atoms is postulated only for the sake of metaphysical consistency and continuity. But does process philosophy allow adequately for the radical diversity among levels of activity in the world and the emergence of genuine novelty at all stages of evolutionary history? Could greater emphasis be given to emergence and the contrasts between events at various levels, while preserving the basic postulate of metaphysical continuity?[9]

Barbour believes that a revision along these lines would be possible, though he does not indicate how he thinks it should be undertaken.

I have previously sought to explain why I am unable to accept process thought as a metaphysical system.[10] I will come to theological issues later, but my philosophical doubts centre on its relationship with science. We have already seen (p. 6) that though physics does not determine metaphysics, it certainly constrains it by conditions of consonance. I cannot see how the punctuated, event-dominated account of process philosophy fits in with what we know about the dynamics of the physical world. It is important to recognize that there is much continuous development in the quantum mechanical description (the Schrödinger equation is a perfectly respectable differential equation), and that discontinuities only occur at those special events, linking quantum and classical phenomena, that we call measurements.[11] A physics appropriate to process thinking might be expected to be formulated in terms of the discrete steps of what mathematicians call difference equations, rather than continuously varying differential equations. That is not how physics is expressed today.

No one can write about topics such as divine or human agency without adopting at least a tacit metaphysical position. That, of course, is as true of the claims of the physical reductionists (who certainly go beyond what science alone has been able to tell them) as it is of the scientist-theologians who resist reductionism. Yet not everyone who ventures into these areas seems willing to lay their metaphysical cards face upwards on the table. I have to say that I feel that Peacocke has always been somewhat reticent about the metaphysical basis of his thought. We shall have to seek to piece together his position from the later discussion of specific issues, most particularly the question of God's action in the world.[12]

My own attempts at sketching a metaphysical stance have proceeded from the conviction that none of the classical positions on the relationship of mind and matter are tenable today. Dualism sits ill with the continuous evolution of a quark soup (the material universe 10^{-10} seconds old) into the home of saints and mathematicians. On its account, mind has to be integrated with material cosmic history at some later stage, in a discontinuous manner. In addition, dualism has never succeeded in describing in a satisfactory fashion how mind and matter can be understood to interact with each other. On the other hand, materialism and idealism fail to do justice to the serious motivations we have for asserting our experience of *both* the material *and* the mental in an even-handed way.

In consequence, I have tried to join with those who seek a dual-aspect monism, a metaphysic in which mind and matter are complementary aspects of one 'world-stuff', perceived (as a physicist would say) in the different phases of the material and the mental.[13] I have had, more than once, ruefully to quote the opinion of Thomas Nagel (who also espouses a dual-aspect monism) that in our present state of incomplete knowledge the dual-aspect claim can amount to 'nothing more than pre-Socratic flailing about'.[14] Nevertheless, one has to do what one can, and there seem to be mildly hopeful directions in which to wave one's hands.

In quantum theory, complementarity succeeds in reconciling characteristics that one would, from a common sense point of view, suppose to be categorically disjoint (e.g. wave and particle). What permits this act of metaphysical legerdemain is the presence of an intrinsic indeterminancy in the situation – a wavelike state contains an *indefinite* number of particles. Here is perhaps the glimmer of a clue of how to make a pre-Socratic sort of guess about mind and matter (likely in its detail to be about as accurate as Thales' belief that the world was made of water – not exactly correct, but it was a fruitful thought that the variety of the world might have a simple underlying substrate). The indefiniteness to which I am inclined to look is intrinsic unpredictability, found not only in the quantum world, but, since chaos theory, recognized also in the everyday classical world as well. How one might hope that this could work out will become clearer in the discussion of agency, where I shall want to consider the concept of 'active information' to set alongside that of energetic causality.

One of the most critical encounters in the science and theology debate occurs in the discussion of God's action in the world. On the one hand, science appears to describe an all-embracing and self-contained causality at work in forming the future from the present, through the outworking of the laws of nature. Religion, on the other hand, wishes to speak of divine activity, on the basis of its experience of response to prayer and its prophetic interpretation of history. How can the two possibly be reconciled? There is encouragement to believe that there must be a way out of this dilemma, for we recognize that too tight a drawing of the net of physical causality alone would also threaten our own experience of intentional agency. While philosophers may question human free will, it seems to me to be the basis for rationality as well as action.[15] What would validate human utterance if it were merely the mouthings of automata?

One proposed strategy for solving the problem of God's action relies on an appeal to divine distance from the detail of the hurly-burly of cosmic process. It can take two forms. One is the quasi-deistic idea that divine agency is to be conceived solely in terms of God's timeless single great act of holding world history in being. The eternal 'Let there be' is the sum of divine action, and there can be no specific concern with particular events within the total account of occurrence. Maurice Wiles has defended such a view.[16] A more positive concept of divine action is proposed by the tradition, from at least St Thomas Aquinas onwards, of speaking of divine primary causality as in some way present, but hidden, within the secondary causalities of the scientific account. A modern proponent, Austin Farrer, wrote of God's agency as able 'to work omnipotently on, in and through creaturely agencies, without either forcing them or competing with them'.[17] This is so mysterious a notion that it effectively removes the question of God's action from discussion in ordinary human conversation.

The 'single act' account assimilates providence to the divine upholding of creation in a way that is inadequate for a God described (no doubt in stretched analogical terms) as personal. If such language is to mean anything, it must surely imply the possibility of particular divine acts on particular occasions, and not just rely on a generality of divine sustaining. The scientist-theologians are not persuaded by Wiles.[18]

Primary causality seems no more than the imposition of a mysterious theological gloss on natural process.[19] Its explanatory power is by no means evident. Peacocke has sometimes taken a view that seems quite close to it:

> Thus we must conceive of God as creating *in* the whole process from beginning to end, through and through, or he cannot be involved at all. It is not so much a question of primary and secondary causes, as classically expounded, but rather the natural, causal, creative nexus of events *is* itself God's creative action.[20]

However, I find myself much more in sympathy when he writes concerning Farrer's account of double agency that 'advocacy of this paradox comes perilously close to the mere assertion of its truth'.[21] Peacocke chides Farrer for being unwilling to discuss the 'causal joint' by which divine action might impinge upon the created world.

The stronger one's account of divine action, the more perplexing must become the problems of evil and suffering in the world. More will be said about this in a later chapter, but it seems to me that the ascription of all that happens to God's primary causality faces this difficulty in a peculiarly acute form. Barbour's comment on these issues is: 'The neo-Thomist position is appealing because it shows great respect for science while maintaining many of the doctrines of classical theism. . . . But it is difficult to reconcile with the biblical idea that God has a more active continuing role in nature and history.'[22]

I think the difficulty is not so much with action (which after all is claimed if not explained), but with an adequate concept of history. Both the approaches that we have been discussing relate God to the totality of cosmic events, laid out before him in time as well as space. Their natural expression is in terms of God's action in a so-called space-time 'block universe'. The latter is a concept that is appropriate to a static world of being, but it is highly problematic in relation to a dynamical world of becoming.[23] We shall return briefly to questions of temporality at the end of this chapter.

The converse of distancing God from the individual events of cosmic history is the strategy of incorporating these events themselves within the divine being. At its most extreme, this would lead to pantheism, but this has had little appeal to the scientist-theologians for it is too reductive of the distinctiveness of God's nature by equating it to that of the physical world. The idea of panentheism has, however, proved more beguiling. One might define this position as stating that the world in some sense exists in God, but that he in his divine nature exceeds the world. Peacocke would deny that this is asserting that the world is part of God,[24] though that would certainly seem to have been implied by the *doyen* of modern panentheistic theologians, Charles Hartshorne, when he wrote that panentheism means that God is 'both this system [the cosmos] and something independent of it'.[25] Both Barbour and Peacocke in their writings have frequently presented themselves as proponents of panentheism. I have consistently opposed it.[26]

Barbour's version of panentheism is articulated in terms of process thought. God is a participant in the prehensive phase of every event, seeking to 'lure' its outcome in a favourable direction. On the other hand, the initiating of the concrescent phase, which brings about a specific outcome, lies with the actual occasion itself. Process theology, therefore, seems to present a very qualified form of panentheism, with a clear distinction remaining between the divine role and the sequence of events that make up the account of physical process. In fact, my theological criticism of process thinking is precisely that it gives an inadequate account of divine action, which seems to be restricted to the role of a powerless pleading from the margins of occurrence. Barbour tells us that process thinkers 'believe in a God of persuasion rather than compulsion', one who 'influences the world without determining it'.[27] In reacting against a God seen as a dominating Cosmic Tyrant, process theologians appear to have settled for a Marginal Persuader. Just as the Tyrant cannot be the God of love, so the Persuader is too much in thrall to his creation to be the Ground of hope. Barbour admits as much when he writes, 'Process theology does call in question the traditional expectation of *an absolute victory over evil*.'[28]

Peacocke at times has written about panentheism in terms that are almost pantheistic in tone: 'God is in all the creative processes of his creation and they are all equally "acts of God" for he is everywhere and at all times present and active in them as their agent.'[29] Yet recently he has said, 'I have not wanted to imply an equally direct involvement of God in all events nor that all events equally and in the same sense affect God – as often appears to be an implication of process theology.'[30] He cites with apparent approval a definition of panentheism as, 'The belief that the Being of God includes and penetrates the whole universe, so that every part of it exists in Him but (as against pantheism) that his Being is more than, and is not exhausted by, the universe', while explaining that his motivation is 'an overt desire to hold together both the transcendence and the immanence of God in relation to the world'.[31] Many of us would share a recognition of the need to correct classical theism's undue emphasis on the transcendent remoteness of God, without feeling that this implied a necessity to adopt panentheistic language. It simply requires a recovery of the balancing orthodox concept of divine immanence.

Another strategy for consideration of questions of agency is to question the tightness with which physics draws its causal net. In the twentieth century we have become aware of the existence of intrinsic unpredictabilities within our account of the physical world. The most famous of these is the probabilistic character of quantum events, which does not permit the determination of a specific outcome on most occasions. To this must be added the discovery of chaotic systems, whose exquisite sensitivity to the fineness of detail of their circumstances imposes severe restrictions on predictability, even in the regime of classical Newtonian physics.[32]

Unpredictability is an epistemological property. It tells us that we cannot know beforehand how such systems will behave. A distinction must be drawn between knowledge of a system and that system's real nature. In consequence, there is no logically necessary way of moving from unpredictability to an ontological statement about how things actually are, such as the assertion of a kind of 'openness' to the future for such systems. Equally, though, there is no logical bar to making such a move as an act of metaphysical conjecture. Epistemology and ontology are distinct from each other, but the strategy of realism is to use the former as the source of reasonable motivation for ideas concerning the latter. In relation to the intrinsic unpredictability of quantum theory, this has been an almost universal strategy. Our inability to measure precisely both the position and the momentum of a quantum entity has been treated not as a defect in knowledge, but as an insight into the nature of the quantum world. Almost all physicists and philosophers treat Heisenberg's uncertainty principle (which initially was an epistemological discovery about what can be measured) as an ontological statement of quantum indeterminancy. Bohm's instructive deterministic interpretation of quantum theory[33] shows us that this is not a forced move, though it has certainly been a popular one.

In the case of chaos theory, there has been greater hesitancy. No doubt, a restraining influence has been the fact that an underlying deterministic interpretation was immediately to hand – in the form of the time-honoured theory of classical mechanics – in contrast to quantum theory, where Bohm's account was only constructed long after the initial discoveries. A non-deterministic interpretation of chaos theory is much more unfamiliar and it has not been worked out in full detail. Nevertheless, I have proposed that this is the interpretation that we should adopt.[34] I shall explain later how I then view the deterministic equations of classical mechanics.

One reason for this move is that it is a natural step to take if science is treated in accord with a critical realist point of view. If epistemology models ontology, then what we know or cannot know is to be treated as an indication of what is actually the case. This is clearly the conviction that underlies the almost universal indeterministic interpretation of quantum theory. I believe that this attitude should encourage us to take a similar stance in relation to the unpredictabilities of chaos theory.

A second reason is that to take this step is to make a move in the direction of beginning to conceive of an account of physical process sufficiently subtle and supple in its character to offer the prospect of accommodating our experiences of human agency. If that is the case, it would be a significant advance for *modern science*, for that discipline would begin for the first time to describe a world of which we can conceive ourselves as being inhabitants. The openness of such a world could not just be at the microscopic level of quantum theory, but it would also have to embrace the macroscopic world. I shall argue that a world of this kind would also be sufficiently flexible to accommodate the concept of divine providential interaction with its history.

The way this interpretation could work out is as follows. To treat epistemological unpredictability as the signal of ontological openness is not to deny that causal principles bring about the future, but to enlarge the scope and character of what those principles might be. Although we do not have a fully articulated theory of this way of interpreting chaotic dynamics, its general shape seems clear. Chaotic systems are not totally disorderly; their future is contained within the confines of possibility represented by a limited range of behaviour called a 'strange attractor'. All such possibilities (i.e. different paths traversing the strange attractor) correspond to the same energy; they differ only in the patterns of behaviour that they represent. Secondly, chaotic systems can never be isolated from their environment because of their extreme sensitivity to any external disturbance, however minimal. There is therefore an inescapable need to discuss them in a holistic context.

Thus we may suppose that the energetic causality, arising from interaction between the parts (which physics describes) will be supplemented by holistic causal principles of a pattern-forming kind, leading to what might be called the idea of 'active information': 'active', because the holistic principle brings about actual future behaviour; 'information', because its action relates to structure rather than to energetic properties. The deterministic equations from which classical chaos theory first developed are then to be understood as 'downward emergent' approximations to the true physical reality, applicable in those rare and specific situations in which the constituents can be treated in isolation from their environment. In general, such isolation is not possible and behaviour depends upon the total situation. I have called this point of view 'contextualism'.[35] It corresponds to a strong form of anti-reductionism in which not only are higher order concepts autonomous because of their irreducibility to constituent language, but the same is also true of higher order processes.[36] The whole is indeed more than the sum of its parts because it exerts an influence on the parts. There is causality that flows from top to bottom, as well as from bottom to top.

In this concept of top-down causality by active information, supplementing the bottom-up causality of energetic interchange between constituents, we can see a pre-Socratic *glimmer* of how mind and matter might interact in a complementary dual-aspect monism. There seems no reason, however, to suppose that such top-down causality acts only in humans or other animate entities. There may well be holistic laws of nature, driving the evolution of complexity, at present unknown to us but in principle discoverable by science. It also seems entirely coherent to suppose that God interacts with creation in the same way. We detect another pre-Socratic glimmer, this time about how theological talk of the Spirit guiding and leading creation might be cashed out within the flexibility of physical process.

Here we might pause and ask whether one might not achieve a similar kind of picture by putting together the widely assumed ontological openness of quantum theory with the undoubted epistemological unpredictability of chaotic systems. After all, the future behaviour of the latter soon comes to depend on a fineness of detail made inaccessible by Heisenberg uncertainty. I will call this 'the hybrid scheme'. My reservations about simply adopting it as the answer to our search for a supple physical theory arise from unresolved problems about how the classical and quantum worlds interlock with each other in general, and about what is the quantum analogue of chaos in particular.[37] These technical difficulties make it uncertain whether the hybrid scheme is a sufficient explanation of openness, but its general character would, in any case, not be different from that already described. Despite the supposed microscopic origin of its openness, its outworking would be amplified into an irreducibly macroscopic form of behaviour. Because of their unisolability, chaotic macrosystems would need an holistic treatment. There would still be a kind of top-down causality at work in them.

It seems important to recognize that top-down causality by itself is not an unproblematic concept. Though we may rightly feel we have direct experience of it through our willed actions, understanding it surely requires the identification of that openness within the bottom-up description alone that then affords room for manoeuvre for such an holistic form of causation. Without such an identification, top-down causality is a mere slogan. Ontological gaps of the necessary kind, identified within the constituent account, are to be distinguished from those patches of current ignorance whose illegitimate exploitation discredited the notion of a God of the (epistemological) gaps. The conjectures discussed above need the critical realist move from epistemology to ontology to give them respectability. They are attempts to achieve a degree of consonance between science's talk of physical process, humanity's experience of agency, and theology's talk of divine providential action, by suggesting, however tentatively, what the causal joint involved might be.

Peacocke has also explored possible connections between unpredictability and top-down causality.[38] Referring to the way in which the behaviour of a sensitive classical system soon depends upon details at the quantum level, he says that it can be

> described as unpredictable in principle with respect to any detailed description of its microscopic properties. ... On a critical realist account of scientific knowledge we can say that such systems *are* indeterminate with respect to these microscopic properties (if not with respect to macroscopic properties of the assembly).[39]

The last reservation appears to refer to such averaged effects as the temperature and pressure of the gas, so that the remark seems to be in the spirit of what I have called the hybrid scheme. At other times, however, Peacocke uses phrases like 'unpredictability, open-endedness and flexibility',[40] without explicitly noting that the first characteristic is epistemological and the second two are ontological. It is necessary to discuss what scheme could make the bridge between epistemology and ontology, and I am not clear what his answer to this is.

In fact, Peacocke thinks that 'unpredictability, open-endedness and flexibility' may 'show that the world we have is the kind that could be the matrix in which free agents could develop'[41] (presumably along the lines sketched above), but he thinks that idea could only be significant in relation to God's action if the same characteristics apply to 'the world as a whole'. Concerning such an idea of divine top-down interaction upon flexible cosmic process, he says, 'Might not this be the correlate of divine freedom in relation to the world?'[42]

Two comments may be made. The first relates to what Peacocke believes is a contrast between his cosmic account of divine action and what he thinks is a microscopic account on my part. Because I referred to chaotic systems' vulnerability to small disturbances, he believes that I suggested that 'God could be conceived of as actually manipulating micro-events within these initiating fluctuations in the natural world in order to produce the results he wills'.[43] It will be clear that this is a most unfortunate misunderstanding of my position. Vulnerability to small disturbances is simply *diagnostic* of that sensitivity to circumstance that means that the system must, in fact, be treated holistically. Peacocke further believes that I would need to assume that God could predict what was unpredictable to us. In fact, God must know things as they really are, and if unpredictability is the signal of an actual ontological openness, then of course God knows that openness as it is, and the other causal principles (including his own providential will) that can act within it. The sensitivity of chaotic systems is such that they rapidly seem to be open to influence 'from the other side of the universe',[44] but I do not think this precludes the possibility of some instances of quasi-localized causality, such as we presumably exercise within our bodies and perhaps as God does within terrestrial history.

The second comment relates to Peacocke's account of top-down causality. His examples, given in analogy,[45] are drawn from considerations of the way in which dissipative systems far from equilibrium can induce spontaneously self-organized patterns of order,[46] and from the way in which boundary conditions (both spatial and temporal) produce effects on the character of systems. Self-organization seems to me to be most illuminating in relation to the generation of complex structures, while agency seems more likely to be related to the much greater dynamical openness to the future possessed by general chaotic systems. A chemical clock, or hexagonal convection cells, are not much of an analogy with intentional action. 'Active information' seems a little nearer, and that is language that Peacocke also wants to use.[47] The influence of boundary conditions is often capable of being understood in terms of a sequence of localized interactions generating patterns of long-range order, and it does not seem to me to be truly top-down but rather sideways. In any case, it is highly problematic how one could consider God as the boundary condition of the universe. I suspect that one motivation for Peacocke's insistence on the cosmic nature of divine action is to distance it from any notion of arbitrary interruption of local physical process.[48] I am attempting to achieve the same release from a merely arbitrary interventionist account by assigning divine action to a hiddenness within the inescapably cloudy unpredictabilities of physical process, interpreted realistically as the sites of ontological openness.

I am prepared to take the risk of making a (pre-Socratic) guess about the causal joint by which top-down causality is brought to bear. An appeal is made to critical realism as an encouragement to a strategy of maximizing the correlation between epistemological constraint and ontological conjecture. Peacocke's[49] appeal to critical realism seems to be rather more as an encouragement to believe that macro and micro levels are both to be taken seriously, and that therefore there must be some consistency between them in a way not wholly spelled out.

Those who, like Peacocke and myself, want to attempt to speak of agency in terms of active information face a common need to discuss how energy and information are related to each other.[50] There are well-known relations from communications theory that seem to specify a minimum energy expenditure for a specified information content. However, this relates to passive information record, which is not the same as pattern-forming active information. Bohm and Hiley[51] discuss this distinction in relation to the 'guiding wave' in their version of quantum mechanics. It retains its ability to influence the motion of the particle, however attenuated the wave may become. While it may be that in embodied beings like ourselves there will still persist some residual degree of correlation between energy and information, it seems coherent to believe that God's action could be in the form of pure active information. This would afford a particular character to divine agency, consonant with theology's insistence that God is pure spirit.

All the scientist-theologians wish to speak of God's action in the world in a way that goes beyond the single act of upholding the universe in being. Providential agency must be continuously at work in a way consistent with the known laws of nature (themselves understood theologically as expressions of God's faithful and unchanging will for his creation). We all refuse the word 'intervention', and accept the word 'interaction', as the way to speak about divine acts. Our proposals for how one may think about God's action are certainly diverse. None can claim definitive status, but all are presented as helpful metaphysical conjectures. Such acts of intellectual daring in the quest for a causal joint seem necessary if we are to go beyond mere fideistic assertion. Peacocke says, 'without some plausible (certainly not mechanistic) account of *how* God might interact with the causal nexus of individual events in the world, including human-brains-in-human-bodies, we cannot with integrity assert that God does, or might, do so'.[52]

We all take extremely seriously the temporality of the physical world, understood as a realm of true becoming in which the future was not totally contained in what is already past. God must be appropriately related to this temporal reality and we concur in wishing to speak of divine temporality as well as divine eternity.[53] Such a dipolar theism is a gift from process thought that has found a much wider acceptance than within the ranks of the process theologians alone. Since God knows things as they are, if the events of the world are truly temporal, then God must surely know not just that they are successive, but he must know them in their actual succession. The question of divine action remains at the top of the agenda for the science and theology debate, the subject of intense discussion and speculation. Conjectures concerning a causal joint are attempts to take both matter and providence seriously.

4
Cosmic Scope: Creation

TO SCIENTISTS, THEOLOGIANS seem very Earth-bound and tied to human culture. The history they mostly survey is the 4,000-year period running from Abraham to the present day. When they speak of 'the world', they usually mean the Earth. Yet the Sun that our planet encircles is just an ordinary star among the more than 100 million million million stars of the observable universe; 4,000 years is the last fiftieth of a second in the 'cosmic day' of 15 billion years. Of course, size and significance are not the same thing. The coming-to-be of self-conscious life on Earth is surely the most remarkable event in the universe's history known to us. The power of culture to transmit information from one generation to another has, over a few thousand years, changed the face of the Earth and the course of terrestrial evolution. Although we are inhabitants of a mere speck of dust floating in a vast universe, that very vastness is itself an indispensable condition for our being here to wonder at it. Modern cosmology recognizes that a universe capable of evolving people must be as big, and as full of matter, as is our world, for only thus could cosmic history last long enough, and cosmic process have the right character, for this fruitful event to happen. It takes 15 billion years to make men and women. It is a process that cannot be hurried and that requires a universe with at least as many stars in it as we observe in our own.

Although the historically changing character of the Earth's seas and land masses, and of its animal life, has been recognized for two centuries, it was only in the 1920s that people realized that the whole universe also had had a history. When Einstein discovered the general theory of relativity in 1915, he soon realized that it would enable him to construct a theory of the universe itself, since linking gravity to the curvature of space made it possible to discuss cosmic space–time structure. Yet in those days it seemed axiomatic that it was a static, unchanging universe that should emerge from the calculations. Since this was not in fact the way it worked out theoretically, Einstein made what he later described as 'the greatest blunder' of his life, by tinkering with the equations to make a static solution possible. Within a few years, however, the theoretical insight of the Russian meteorologist, Alexander Friedman, and the Belgian priest, Georges Lemaître, and the observational discoveries of the American astronomer, Edwin Hubble, had led to what we now call 'big bang cosmology'. The steady-state theory of Bondi, Gold and Hoyle was proposed in 1948 in a conscious attempt to return to an everlastingly unchanging picture of the universe. The discovery of the background radiation (a kind of lingering echo of the big bang) has resulted in the abandonment of steady-state ideas by almost all cosmologists.

These discoveries have greatly enlarged our concept of what it means to speak of an evolutionary world. Biological evolution on Earth had to be preceded by 10 billion years of stellar evolution, in whose course the heavier elements that would constitute the chemical basis of life were formed in the nuclear furnaces of the stars. These elements were then made available by being scattered into the environment through supernovae explosions. The universe is intrinsically dynamic. Nowhere does this seem to be more true than in the immediate aftermath of the big bang itself. Within a fraction of a second of the initiating event, cosmologists believe that a bewildering sequence of cosmic transformations took place, greatly expanding and smoothing the universe and breaking down the ur-force of the fundamental, highly symmetrical, grand unified theory into the asymmetrical variety of the forces of nature that we observe today.

The scientist-theologians are well aware of the temporal and spatial setting in which the human story unfolds. They wish to take it seriously, particularly in relation to the theological doctrine of creation. A persistent problem in discussions with agnostic scientist colleagues is to get the latter to recognize that creation is not the answer to the temporal question 'How did things begin?', but to the ontological question 'Why does anything exist?' I have reproved Stephen Hawking for naïveté in supposing that, were his speculations that the universe has a finite age but no dateable beginning to prove to be correct, this would somehow make the Creator redundant.[1] God is not there just to start things off. Hawking is nearer the mark when he asks, in relation to a supposed grand unified theory, 'What is it that breathes fire into the equations and makes a universe for them to describe?'[2] The central concept of the doctrine of creation is divine ordaining and sustaining, not divine initiation.

Central to a modern doctrine of creation must be the recognition of the evolutionary character of the universe. Peacocke is absolutely right to say that 'any doctrine of creation, if it is not to become vacuous and sterile, must be about the relation of God to, and the creation by God of, the world which the natural sciences describe'.[3] Christian thinkers like Charles Kingsley and Aubrey Moore reacted positively to Charles Darwin's insights, and there has been more than a century of fruitful endeavour to understand how an evolutionary world can be understood as a created world. A particularly positive and clear contribution has been made by Peacocke.[4] As befits a biochemist, his principal concern has been with biological evolution, but the ideas presented readily extend to the wider cosmic evolutionary scene. The other scientist-theologians have also made their contributions to this discussion.[5]

A concept of central importance in relation to an evolutionary world is that of *creatio continua*, continuing creation.[6] God's relation to the universe is at *all* times that of its Creator, and fruitful evolutionary history must be understood theologically as the expression and fulfilment of his purpose. There is no tension here with the doctrine of *creatio ex nihilo*, for the latter affirms that it is God's will alone that holds all in being. A full concept of creation requires the ideas both of God's timeless sustaining (creation out of nothing) and of God's temporal creativity (continuous creation). 'The two are respectively the transcendent and immanent poles of divine creativity.'[7] However, talk of *creatio continua* must be more than the imposition of a pious gloss upon physical process. If the phrase is to have real meaning, then the divine will must actually be at work within the particularities of cosmic history. Hence the importance of a more than minimal account of God's action, which we discussed in the preceding chapter. The theological language found to be well adapted to the discrete but effective participation of the Creator in the fulfilment of creation is that relating to the hidden working of the Spirit.[8] The motivation for the use of such language lies partly in the astonishing thrust towards evolving complexity, which has turned a ball of energy into the home of humanity in the 15 billion years of cosmic evolution. This fertile phenomenon has impressed those scientists writing from outside any religious tradition.[9]

One could summarize the theological significance of an evolutionary universe as its being a world allowed by its Creator to make itself. Doubtless, God could have produced a ready-made world, but he has done something cleverer than that in allowing creation's history to be the exploration and realization of its God-given fruitfulness. That is, surely, the right way to put it. I am not happy when Peacocke talks about God as involved in exploring through creation,[10] as if he were using the universe as a kind of analogue computer to find out the consequences of the laws and circumstances he has ordained. It is *creation* that is 'discovering' the potentialities with which it has been endowed.

An important point about that evolutionary exploration is that it is the result of a divine letting-be and not the unfolding of an inexorable divine plan. The openness of physical process, about which we spoke in the last chapter, implies that the cosmic drama is the acting out of improvisations and not the reading of a fixed script. God interacts with creation, but he does not overrule it. All the scientist-theologians wish to emphasize the insight that God's act of creation involves a kenotic act of self-limitation, truly allowing the other to be. It is therefore necessarily a costly and vulnerable action in which divine almightiness is qualified by the loving gift of an appropriate degree of independence to the beloved creature.[11] We all refer to the writing of W. H. Vanstone. Although his thought is motivated by a profound meditation on the nature of creation by love and it shows no sign of an engagement with modern science, it has led him to give what is a perfect insight into the nature of an evolutionary universe: 'it is the realization of vision, but of vision which is discovered only through its own realization'.[12]

A popular scientific way of referring to the orderly openness of cosmic history is to refer to the interplay of 'chance and necessity'. By 'chance' is meant happenstance, the fact that this happens rather than that. It represents a kind of shuffling exploration of possibility. This particular genetic mutation produces this particular possibility for new life, while other mutations do not occur and so other possibilities remain unrealized. By 'necessity' is meant the natural orderliness of the physical world. The relatively reliable transmission of genetic information from one generation to the next permits the preservation of new forms of life. These new forms flourish if they prove advantageously adapted to their lawful environment. Thus regularity sifts the offerings of happenstance. Chance is the engine of novelty in an evolutionary world; necessity is the selector and guardian of fruitfulness. A world of pure chance would be chaotically infertile; a world of pure necessity would be rigidly infertile. It is the interplay of the two tendencies that produces the actual fruitfulness of our universe. Although my illustration has been drawn from biology, exactly the same considerations apply to all stages of evolutionary history.

The word that has given rise to difficulty and misunderstanding is the slippery word 'chance'. Its use in the slogan we are discussing is to represent historical contingency. It is certainly the case that an evolutionary universe is sufficiently flexible and potentially fruitful, for its finite history to represent only a selection of the possible outcomes that might have occurred. We have already recognized that an evolutionary universe is one that, within limits, is making itself rather than executing a predetermined plan. Certain writers, however, such as Jacques Monod[13] and Richard Dawkins,[14] have seized on chance and annexed to it the tendentious adjective 'blind'. They claim that a world of chance and necessity is one that is devoid of any meaning or purpose within its history. This is clearly a metaphysical claim that should not be presented as if it were a scientific conclusion. It is interesting that in their desire to reach this assessment, these authors totally neglect the very remarkable and particular form that 'necessity' must take if cosmic processes are actually to be fruitful. I will discuss anthropic 'fine tuning' a little later on.

The scientist-theologians have resisted this debasing of contingency into randomness. They seek to offer a more positive evaluation of the role of chance, seen as the means for realizing fruitfulness. Peacocke says that the potentialities of the world are 'unveiled by chance exploring their gamut', and he goes on to compare evolution to the improvised development of a great fugue.[15] The recognition of a degree of historical contingency in the details of what is happening does not negate the claim that a creatorly purpose is nevertheless being fulfilled within an evolutionary universe. I do not suppose that the anatomy of Homo sapiens was laid down by an eternal divine decree, but that the world has proved capable of evolving self-conscious worshipping beings seems to have been built into its physical fabric from the start. Theological reflection upon *creatio continua* has to steer a path between two unacceptable extremes – on the one hand, avoiding the rigidity of an inexorable blueprint for the predestination of cosmic history; on the other hand, avoiding the *laissez-faire* world of the Deistic Spectator. God – 'an Improviser of unsurpassed ingenuity' in Peacocke's striking phrase[16] – may well bring about his purposed ends by contingent paths. The role of chance can be seen as a signal of the Creator's allowing his creation to make itself; the role of necessity can be seen as a signal of the Creator's beneficent purposes for his creation. I have written as follows:

> The Christian God is both loving and faithful. The gift of the God of love to his creation will surely be freedom. He will prove to be no Cosmic Tyrant, holding all in tight control. ... The gift of the God of faithfulness will surely be reli-

> ability. He will prove to be no Cosmic Lord of Misrule. ... We may expect the creation of the God who is both loving and faithful to display characteristics of both openness and regularity, such as are in fact reflected in the physical interplay of chance and necessity in the process of the world.[17]

The process of evolution is not a smooth progression. It necessarily involves blind alleys and extinctions. In Vanstone's perceptive words:

> The activity of God in creation must be precarious. It must proceed by no assured programme. Its progress, like every progress of love, must be an angular process – in which each step is a precarious step into the unknown; in which each triumph contains a new potential of tragedy, and each tragedy may be redeemed into a wider triumph.[18]

Exactly the same biochemical processes that allow cells to mutate and produce new forms of life will allow other cells to mutate and become malignant. The presence of cancer in an evolving creation is part of its necessary cost. It is neither a gratuitous horror nor the product of creatorly incompetence. Here science offers a profoundly helpful insight to theology, as the latter wrestles with the problem of the existence of suffering on the scale that we experience it. I am greatly moved by the frequency with which this problem of suffering surfaces in the discussion period following a lecture on science and theology, and I am grateful that there is something useful to be said from the scientific perspective. Of course, I am not suggesting that all perplexities and sorrows are thereby removed. There remains a deep mystery about individual destiny in this regard. The happenstance of the world can be extremely painful and diminishing, but it is at least delivered from being seen as the express imposition of the divine will.

The scientist-theologians recognize this contribution that they can seek to make to theodicy, and it has been a persistent theme in my own writing.[19] Barbour approaches the issue from the perspective of process thought, in which God influences the world but does not determine it, and in which his role is that of the Great Companion in suffering. Opposing the idea that everything is brought about by God's direct control, he says, 'There have been too many blind alleys and extinct species and too much waste, suffering, and evil to attribute every event to God's specific will.'[20] Peacocke also wishes to speak of God's participation in the suffering of creation.[21] Concerning the presence of pain in the world, he writes that 'from a purely naturalistic viewpoint, the emergence of pain and its compounding as suffering as consciousness increases seem to be inevitable aspects of any conceivable developmental process that would be characterized by a continuous increase in ability to process information coming from the environment'.[22] Once again it is being suggested that physical evil is the necessary cost of fruitful complexity. God is not indifferent to the pains of his creation and so Peacocke speaks of a suffering God.[23]

I too wish to speak of the divine acceptance of vulnerability in the self-limiting act of creation. 'Once God is acknowledged to be vulnerable through his love for his creation, it becomes possible to speak of the mystery of a suffering God.'[24] In relation to the existence of physical evil, I have sought to frame a 'free-process defence',[25] in analogy with the familiar free-will defence in relation to moral evil. God allows tectonic plates to slip and cause earthquakes, and bacteria to multiply and cause disease, because they are 'free' to act in accordance with their natures, just as we are free to act in accordance with our nature. Such a world is of greater excellence than would be a rigidly mechanical creation under tight divine control. To those who object that it is an abuse of language to use the adjective 'free' in relation to non-moral entities, I reply that I suspect that there is a relationship, within the interconnectedness of the created order, between the opennesses to the future allowed to non-human and to human creatures:

> The physical universe, with its physical evil, is not just the backdrop against which the human drama, with its moral evil, is being played out, so that the two can be disentangled. We are characters who have emerged from the scenery; its nature is the ground of the possibility of our nature. Perhaps

> only a world endowed with both its own spontaneity and its own reliability could have given rise to beings able to exercise choice. I think it is likely that only a universe in which we could entertain a free-process defence, would be one in which there could be people to whom the free-will defence could be applied.[26]

I have summarized my position by saying, 'God no more expressly wills the growth of a cancer than he expressly wills the act of a murderer, but he allows both to happen. He is not the puppetmaster of either men or matter.'[27]

It is now time to remind ourselves of the modern scientific insight, usually called the Anthropic Principle,[28] that a universe capable of producing beings of the complexity of humankind must be very particular in the given character of the scientific laws that specify its physical fabric. Evolution by itself is not enough to produce fruitfulness; it has to operate in a suitably 'finely tuned' natural environment. Necessity must take a tightly circumscribed form if its interplay with chance is to produce an interesting and fertile cosmic history.

Consideration of the rapid transformations in the very early universe, and of the role of the stars as the sources of energy and also of those heavier elements that are the chemical raw materials of life, together with analyses of the form of terrestrial processes, which depend upon such factors as the anomalous property that ice floats on water, all lead to the conclusion that small variations in the character and strengths of the forces of nature would have rendered the universe subject to a sterility that no amount of the evolutionary interplay of chance and necessity could possibly have overcome. There has been much discussion of the significance that might be attributed to this remarkable insight of modern cosmology.

John Leslie[29] has proposed that the requirement of anthropic precision needs an explanation and that it is not just to be treated as a fortunate fact calling for no further discussion. He thinks that there are broadly two possible ways of making the Anthropic Principle intelligible: an ensemble of universes or a divine design. In the first case, there is supposed to be a vast portfolio of actually existing different worlds, each with a different physical fabric, and we live in the one where, by chance, the anthropic conditions are satisfied because, of course, we could not otherwise have appeared within its history. In the second case, the world is the way it is because a Creator has willed that it should satisfy the conditions necessary for its purposed fruitfulness. In relation to the Anthropic Principle, Leslie regards these metaphysical propositions as being of equal plausibility: 'much evidence suggests that Life's prerequisites could only amazingly have been fulfilled anywhere unless this is a truth: *that God is real and/or there exist many, very varied, universes*'.[30] Peacocke has been anxious to stress the possibility represented by choosing the option 'and' in that italicized passage.[31] I suppose his stance accords with his notion of a divine 'exploring' of possibility. Barbour, rather characteristically, gives a clear account of various options without committing himself to a particular interpretation,[32] other than acknowledging that there is no *demonstration* of God's existence to be had from the argument (no reflective commentator, in fact, appears to claim that there is).

I have seen the Anthropic Principle as being a component in a revised and revived form of natural theology,[33] which seeks to offer insight rather than proof and which appeals to the given physical fabric of the universe (which science assumes) and not to occurrences within its evolving history (which it is science's role to seek to explain). I have sought to find a middle way between the interpretations of the Anthropic Principle that are labelled, respectively, 'weak' and 'strong'.[34] The former interpretation amounts to no more than recognizing the tautology that the state of our universe must be consistent with our being here to observe it. It fails, however, to take into account how remarkably special that state has to be in relation to all the possible universes that we can readily imagine. The 'strong' interpretation proposes that the universe *has* to be capable of producing observers like ourselves. This seems far too strong a teleological assertion for it to be a scientific statement. If, on the other hand, it is a metaphysical proposition that is being advanced, then it presents a teleological requirement whose plausibility would seem to have to rely upon the notion of a Purpose at work in cosmic history. I have proposed a 'Moderate Anthropic Principle, which notes the contingent fruitfulness of the universe as being a fact of interest calling for an explanation'.[35] I concluded that 'there is indeed a meta-question arising from Anthropic Principle considerations to which theism provides a persuasive (but not logically coercive) answer'.[36] I accept Leslie's assessment of the even-handed probability *on its own* of either a many-universes or a theistic interpretation, but regard the latter as being made more probable by other considerations of natural theology that can be added to it.

Another such part of the case for the revived and revised natural theology that I have wished to press, relates to the rational transparency of the universe, the deep accessibility that our minds have to the beautiful order displayed in the cosmos.[37] Central to this insight is the 'unreasonable effectiveness of mathematics' (Eugene Wigner) – that is, the way in which, time and again, the search for beautiful equations has proved to be the key to fruitful advance in fundamental physics. Einstein discovered general relativity precisely through such a quest for mathematical beauty. This profound human ability to understand the world makes science possible and goes far beyond any evolved capacity needed in the struggle for survival in the everyday world of direct human experience. 'The physical universe seems shot through with signs of mind. That is indeed so, says the theist, for it is God's Mind that lies behind its rational beauty.'[38] This is not a theme that my colleagues have developed to any extent, but it is certainly one that makes an impact on someone whose scientific experience has lain in fundamental physics.

The most significant questions for theology arising from cosmic process are those relating to the future rather than the past. How will it all end? In a word, one can say 'badly'. In our immediate locality, in 5 billion years' time, the Sun will have consumed all its hydrogen fuel and it will then turn into a grossly swollen red giant, burning up any surviving life on Earth. Taking a broader view, the whole universe will either collapse back into a 'big crunch' or decay into low grade radiation, according to whether gravity or expansion is found to dominate its history. (We do not know enough at present to be able to predict which of these two possibilities will be realized.) Either way, the cosmos is condemned to eventual futility. The scientist-theologians fully recognize the challenge this presents to claims that a divine purpose is at work in creation.[39]

The atheist cosmologist, Frank Tipler,[40] has offered the idea of what he calls 'a physical eschatology'. Although carbon-based life is condemned to eventual extinction, maybe intelligence will engineer its own successors, embodied in increasingly novel ways, until, in the closing split seconds of a collapsing universe, the whole cosmos is an ever-faster racing computer of ultimately infinite processing-power. Thus final if fleeting fulfilment would be achieved by this coming-to-be of an infinite 'intelligence'. Tipler calls this the creation of an evolved 'god', and believes that this bizarre proposal can be facilitated by the imposition of a particular end-state boundary condition upon the quantum cosmological description of the universe.

The scientist-theologians are not impressed by such highly speculative proposals. Barbour says that 'they reflect views of humanity, God and the future that are at odds with basic biblical convictions'. The person is not 'a purely rational intellect defined by information-processing ability'.[41] Tipler proposed that his 'god'-like cosmic computer would 'recreate' ourselves and past history as simulations in its software. Peacocke points out that even if this were possible, it would recreate past evil as much as past good, and comments, 'There can be no hope there.'[42] I described the proposal as 'fantastic and curiously chilling', saying that, 'In religious terms, it corresponds to a kind of cosmic tower of Babel, the fundamental error of confounding creation with its Creator. I regard physical eschatology as presenting us with the ultimate *reductio ad absurdum* of a merely evolutionary optimism.'[43]

Where, then, can hope be located? The believer's answer must be, 'in the faithfulness of God alone'. For Barbour, his adherence to process thought implies that this will find expression through the preservation of present achievement by its everlasting remembrance in the mind of God.

> *Objective immortality* is our participation in God's consequent nature, whereby God's life is permanently enriched. Our lives are meaningful because they are preserved everlastingly in God's experience, in which evil is transmuted and the good is saved and woven into the harmony of the larger whole. God's goal is not the completed achievement of a static final realm, but rather a continuing advance towards richer and more harmonious relationships.[44]

He goes on to consider the possibility of a '*subjective immortality*, in which the human self continues as a centre of experience in a radically different environment but amid continuing change rather than a changeless environment'.[45] Whitehead considered this as being consistent with his metaphysics, though he did not himself go beyond the hope of an objective immortality. Barbour's own view is not made clear.

However speculative our thought must be about the nature of a cosmic destiny beyond the collapse or decay of the present universe, and about the nature of our own destiny beyond our deaths, it seems to me that trust in the ever-faithful God is indeed the foundation for such an expectation (see Mark 12. 26–7). The pursuit of consonance between theology and science requires us to endeavour to make such sense of it as we can, though our thought must clearly go beyond what unaided science can afford us. This task has been a recurring theme in my writing.[46] It seems to me that it is the essence of humanity to be embodied and that the soul is the immensely complex 'information-bearing pattern' in which the ever-changing atoms of our bodies are arranged. It is surely a coherent hope that the pattern that is me will be remembered and re-embodied by God in his eschatological act of resurrection. The 'matter' of that resurrected world will be the transformed matter of this dying universe, transmuted by God in his faithful action of cosmic resurrection. It will have new properties, consistent with the end of transience, death and suffering, because it will be part of a new creation, now no longer standing apart from it Çreator as the 'other', and so paying the necessary cost of an evolutionary world's making of itself, but fully integrated with the divine life through the universal reconciliation brought about by the Cosmic Christ (see Col. 1.20). The whole universe will have become sacramental, infused with the divine life. One can say that 'panentheism is true as an eschatological fulfilment, not a present reality'.[47]

These are deeply mysterious ideas, but not, I think, incoherent ideas. Their most perspicuous lodging in Christian experience is the resurrection of Christ, that seminal act from which this new creation has already begun to grow. The empty tomb is of great importance, 'with its proclamation that the risen Lord's glorified body is the transmutation of his dead body; that in Christ there is a destiny not only for humanity but also for matter'.[48]

If it is intrinsic to humankind to be embodied in some way, then it is surely also intrinsic to be temporal. In modern scientific understanding, matter, space and time all go together. Thus human destiny is not a timeless eternity but an everlasting and dynamic exploration of the inexhaustible riches of the divine nature, made accessible in that God-filled world to come. This hope is not unlike Barbour's description of subjective immortality.

Peacocke also wishes to speak of the ultimate fulfilment of creation as lying in *theosis*, a sharing in the divine life.[49] He finds that Dante's *Paradiso* presents a moving image of this theme, but he has little to say about how he envisages that this eschatological destiny can be accommodated within the consonance demanded by the dialogue of science and theology.

The scientist-theologians agree in seeing the evolutionary history of the universe as being compatible with its interpretation as God's action of continuing creation. They acknowledge the role of chance (the contingencies of happenstance), but deny that this destroys the possibility of meaning. Instead they interpret it as a reflection of the divine letting-be, the self-restriction of God's power in the act of permitting the truly other to exist. A world of this kind, allowed to make itself, has a necessary cost in the blind alleys and malfunctions that inevitably accompany evolutionary history. We all find here some help with the problem of physical evil, and it leads us to speak, in somewhat different ways, of God's participation in the sufferings of creation.

I have particularly wanted to emphasize that the recognition that the form of necessity corresponding to the fact that the laws of nature must be 'fine tuned' for an anthropically fruitful universe provides a component in a revived and revised natural theology, to which the insight of the universe's deep rational intelligibility also contributes.

The scientist-theologians all recognize that the eventual futility of cosmic history poses a problem that theology must take seriously. A speculative 'physical eschatology' is not welcomed as the solution being sought. For our part, we make differing responses to this challenge. It has been a major concern in my own writing, for I believe that a credible eschatology is essential for the coherence of Christian belief.

5
Ecumenical Embrace: World Faiths

MODERN SCIENCE FIRST developed in Western Europe. Its inauguration required an expectation not only that the natural world was orderly, but also that the order with which it was endowed was one that could not be discovered by pure thought alone. It was necessary to observe the world to discover the patterns of its actual regularity. Some historians have suggested that it was the Judaeo-Christian-Islamic theological tradition of belief in God the Creator that provided the ideological matrix in which modern science could come to birth.[1] Because God is rational, his creation will be lawfully regular; because God is free, his creation's order will be contingent on what the Creator had in fact chosen to bring into being. One has to look to see what he has done.

Whatever merit there is in this thesis (and it certainly makes some points worth thinking about), it is clearly the case that the subsequent practice of science has not been restricted to the lands of its origin. It has proved eminently exportable. Today science flourishes in countries like India and Japan, just as it does in Europe and in Europe's intellectual offspring, North America. The contrast with the impact world-wide of the Middle Eastern religions is striking. The historic faith traditions of East Asia have proved stable and resistant to missionary endeavours. Only in Africa, and in Christianity's case in South America, and for Islam in India, have Christianity and Islam made substantial inroads into indigenous religion, but even there it is clear that native influences have often remained powerful beneath the surface. Among themselves, the Middle Eastern religions have each proved relatively stable in commanding the support of their adherents.

The triumph of science has not been absolutely universal,

and there are Westerners who point to an alternative wisdom about humanity's attitude to nature, which they believe is preserved in the thinking of native Americans and the aboriginal peoples of Australasia. Nevertheless, the widespread acceptance of modern science is manifest. Does not the contrasting regionalism of religion suggest that the latter is a cultural construct rather than a path of universal access to reality? Theology generally, and the science and theology debate in particular, cannot be conducted in the late twentieth century without an acute awareness of the diversity, stability and apparent dissonance of the great faith traditions of the world.

All the scientist-theologians are aware of the problems that this presents.[2] We all wish respectfully to acknowledge the presence of authentic and deep spiritual experience within the other faiths, while taking our own stand within the tradition of Christianity. Barbour says, 'Each heritage seems to have its characteristic strengths and weaknesses, its particular virtues and temptations ... my main task is to respond to the deepest insights of my own heritage.'[3] Peacocke, for his part, states his policy as being that 'a Western writer seeking to interpret the religious experience of human beings to a Western readership could do best with reference to their common Christian inheritance ... but in no way is this meant to imply that other non-Christian religions cannot be a path to that reality which is, as I shall argue, God'.[4] I share the desire not to proclaim the exclusive victory of total Christian truth over other religions' supposed total error. We have things to learn from each other. However, I am anxious to state my own position in a way that is, perhaps, clearer in rejecting a merely cultural specificity about my Christian faith. That there is an *element* of cultural influence is clear – 'If I had grown up in Saudi Arabia, rather than in England, it would be foolish to deny that the chances are I would be a Muslim. But the chances are also that I would not have spent most of my life as a theoretical physicist'[5] – but that is only part of the story:

> We certainly do not want to be triumphalist, but nor do we wish to forget that there may well be issues on which we are

> right and those who do not share our view are mistaken. In the end, it is the question of truth that matters, and there is an inevitable exclusivity about truth. If you tell me that you hold the view that the phenomenon of heat is due to the subtle fluid caloric, I do not say that you are entitled to your opinion and I respect you for it. I try, instead, to convince you of the correctness of the kinetic theory of heat energy. Either Jesus is God's Lord and Christ or he is not, and it matters supremely to know which is the right judgement.[6]

If religion were simply a means of inculcating a way of life, then there would be no great perplexity about the diversity of its expression. Different cultures produce different styles. What suits one will not necessarily suit another. Indeed, one might welcome a portfolio of different practices from which to select the one most tailored to one's own personal needs. Within each faith tradition, we see exactly this happening. There are ways of negation and ways of affirmation, the life of the ascetic, of the mystic, of the ordinary worshipper whose life is necessarily in the world. Yet these different manners of life are conducted within one tradition that serves not only to encourage such practice, but also to do so on the basis of certain shared cognitive claims about the nature of ultimate reality. When we compare one faith tradition with another, we necessarily encounter the dissonance between their different cognitive assertions.

Barbour and I are both very conscious of the problems that this welter of competing and incompatible religious claims presents to us.[7] He notes, without further comment, the clash of views about the significance of suffering, a problem with which Christianity continually wrestles, but which is regarded by Buddhism and Hinduism as the result of the deserved outworking of the impersonal law of *karma*.[8] Barbour believes that 'differences between integral religious traditions – Hinduism and Christianity, for example – are so great that they can best be understood as the product of different *paradigms*'.[9] He is appealing here to the notion, introduced by Thomas Kuhn into the philosophy of science, of a paradigm or total world view within which reality is surveyed. Barbour regards a paradigm as 'a tradition embodied in historical exemplars'.[10] This may be a useful way of describing the situation, but it does not itself resolve the issue of truth claims made by the competing paradigms. Barbour's conclusion is not encouraging to the concept of a convergence of religious understandings:

> There are no rules for deciding when to abandon a paradigm in science, but *an eventual consensus emerges* – even though there may be rival paradigms for protracted periods, and no paradigm can be considered permanent. The emergence of consensus in religion seems an unrealizable goal. There are differences in cultural context which are intertwined with religious beliefs; hopefully any future global civilization will preserve considerable cultural diversity, and with it, religious pluralism.[11]

In his Gifford lectures, Barbour argues for what he calls 'Pluralistic Dialogue', a position that he acknowledges may 'end closer to relativism than to absolutism'. Yet he also says, 'Pluralistic Dialogue allows us to give pre-eminence to revelation and salvation in Christ without denying the possibility of revelation or salvation in other traditions.'[12] He recognizes that there are necessary limits to Pluralistic Dialogue's acceptance of mutual coexistence: 'We cannot avoid passing judgments on cannibalism, Satanism or Nazism or raising questions about what we see as the inadequacies of other religious traditions.'[13] Barbour feels that the recognition that theologies necessarily trade in models, and not in absolutely adequate descriptions, is helpful to inter-faith dialogue. 'The recognition that models are not pictures of reality can contribute to tolerance between religious communities.'[14]

Pluralist Dialogue has some kinship with the stance on inter-faith matters that is often called 'inclusivism', though the latter places a clearer emphasis in the uniqueness, and not just pre-eminence, of Christ. Inclusivism is my own position, for which I am happy to adopt the definition proposed by Gavin D'Costa: 'one that affirms the salvific presence of God in non-Christian religions while still maintaining that Christ is the definitive and authoritative revelation of God'.[15] If that is the case, we encounter the diversity of the world's faith traditions with respect, but not with complacency. Their clashing claims about reality have to be addressed and not just accepted.

In my sketch of these differences, I too have referred to different evaluations of suffering, placing emphasis on the Christian interpretation of the cross of Christ as a literal participation by God in the human situation, as a fellow-sufferer and not merely a compassionate spectator.[16] Even the religions of the Middle East, despite the commonalities resulting from their linked histories, make profound, conflicting, non-negotiable assertions: Judaism's claim for Israel's unique and continuing status as God's chosen people; Christianity's claim that Jesus is God's incarnate Son; Islam's claim of the infallible authority of the divinely dictated Qur'an.[17] They are surely all seeking to speak of the same God, but they do so with very different voices. When we come to the religions of East Asia, the contrasts become much more extreme and perplexing.[18] There is, for example, the question of the status of the individual self: of unique value or ultimately an illusion? The writers I have found most helpful are those who approach the other religions with a sympathetic openness, which is nevertheless rooted in a clearly articulated Christian understanding.[19] I must hold to the truth of my heritage: 'The Christian hope lies not in the attainment of non-desire, but in the purification that leads to right desire.'[20]

The serious encounter of the world faith traditions is still at an early stage. Years, probably centuries, of dialogue lie ahead. As we begin to enter into that dialogue we would do well to remember Max Warren's words: 'Our first task in approaching another people, another culture, another religion, is to take off our shoes, for the place we are approaching is holy.'[21] We shall need to meet each other, not seeking a facile and unrealistic reduction to a vague and unrecognizable lowest common denominator, still less desiring to vanquish in argument those who differ from us, but wishing firmly but respectfully to offer the riches of insight and experience that our tradition has given us. Our initial meeting places will have to be at the peripheries of our traditions, for encounter at the heart of each faith would be too fraught with threat and it could lead to a painful defensiveness. I have suggested that it is here that the science and theology debate can hope to make a modest contribution.[22]

The scientist, describing a physical reality that is profoundly rational and whose evolving fruitfulness has depended upon an anthropic 'fine tuning' of the fabric of the universe, is giving an account of a world that is readily consonant with the religious traditions of the Middle East, which share a realist understanding of a created universe. We need to ask our colleagues from the Hindu and Buddhist traditions, which to occidentals seem to take a less realist view with their talk of the play of *maya* (illusion), how they see these matters. The suggestions that have been made that quantum physics is more consonant with Eastern than with Western thought[23] have mostly originated from Western interpreters of those traditions. It would be of great interest to learn what assessments might be made by those who have lived wholly within the indigenous heritage and practice of these oriental faiths.

Another potential meeting place for dialogue is provided by contrasting attitudes to the nature of time.[24] The Middle Eastern religions take a strongly linear and progressive view of time (a path to be trodden), while the East Asian religions appear to view it in more cyclical terms (a samsaric wheel from which to seek release). The former seems the more consonant with science's description of an evolving world of becoming, endowed with an arrow of time. The Hindu and Buddhist scriptures speak of vast aeons of time (in contrast to the short time scales of Middle Eastern scriptures), in which the world successively comes into being and goes out of being. Some have seen here an analogy with highly speculative cosmologies that suppose that the physical universe may have gone through 'breathing modes' of successive expansion and collapse, of big bang followed by big crunch, followed by a further big bang, etc. In these, and perhaps other small ways, the interaction of science and theology may contribute to the interacting of the world faiths.

The scientist-theologians are aware of the contrast between global science and regional religion. They recognize both the presence of widespread and authentic spiritual experience in the great faith traditions of the world, and also the clash of cognitive claims that the different religions' understandings represent. No simple resolution of these perplexities is to be had, but contrasting approaches to the nature of the physical world may offer some opportunity for dialogue. The pursuit of truth requires a continuing engagement with inter-faith issues. The brevity of this chapter indicates how much remains to be done.

6
Particularity: Christian Belief

RELIGIONS ARE ROOTED in particularity. They appeal to foundtional events and persons. They express themselves through oft-repeated stories, conveyed and reflected upon within the faith community. In part, this corresponds to the necessary uniqueness inherent in personal encounter. The seminal events of a tradition may be reported. They may, by the process that theologians call *anamnesis* (by which the past comes to be made alive in the present), be re-presented in a liturgical setting (Passover, the Eucharist), but they cannot be repeated. This particularity is a concept not totally foreign to science. While most experimental investigations can be recapitulated, there are unique regimes (such as the highly energetic universe in the split seconds following the big bang) and unique histories (such as biological evolution) that also cannot be repeated. They must be understood in their specificity, and in that mode they are the source of considerable illumination.[1] The scientist-theologians all write from within the specificities of the Christian tradition.

One way to identify the particularity of a religious tradition is to consider those writings that it treats as scripture – that is to say, as authoritative and normative in relation to the belief and practice of that religion. The Christian scriptures are an essential resource for the scientist-theologians. Like all scripture, the Bible functions in two ways: as an evidential record of the foundational events and persons of the tradition, and as the collection of writings, including stories (whether historical or not), that convey the patterns of understanding and commitment that the tradition embodies. When we read the Bible in the first mode, we are submitting it to our interrogation and judgement. When we read the Bible in the second mode, we are submitting ourselves to its interrogation and judgement. Both modes are necessary for a truthful engagement with the reality of religion. The first approach may be called historical, the second mythical, *provided* it is understood that the latter word is not being used in a debased modern sense to mean simply what is untrue. Religious myth is a form of story that is a prime vehicle for conveying religious truth, and it is not the negation of what is historical. It may or may not be an actually enacted story. In fact, Christianity, with its concern for the universal saving significance of a particular life and death (and resurrection) in first-century Palestine, is precisely concerned with the union of the mythical and the historical. 'The power of myth and the power of actuality fuse in the incarnation. . . . The centre of Christianity lies in the *realized myth* of the incarnation.'[2]

Scripture is very important to me in my own attempts at theological thinking, and I have, perhaps, written more explicitly about its role than the other scientist-theologians have done, though we all have a concern with the Bible.[3] As one reads the Bible, one must seek to be true to its nature, which is certainly not that of a divinely guaranteed textbook in which we can look up all the answers. Rather, it is 'a prime means by which we come to know God's dealings with humankind and particularly his self-utterance in Christ'.[4] The fact that the Gospels, and other biblical narratives, are already interpreted accounts does not surprise the scientist, whose experiments must also deal in interpreted facts and not merely raw observations. Of course, the writers of Scripture lived in a world whose thought in many respects, not least scientific, was very different from our own today. Timeless divine truth and timebound cultural expression are intertwined in the biblical pages. Nevertheless, it is a fact of experience that Scripture can speak to us across the centuries. I believe that the best model for comprehending this power to transcend historical limitation is provided for us by the idea of a 'classic', for which Shakespeare and the Greek dramatists provide further examples.[5] Symbolic significance and historical enactment, the inspirational and the evidential, are interwoven into the fabric of the Bible. 'Symbol is not to be reduced to sign by an insistence that it carry a single univocal meaning. Equally the Bible is not to be tied down; it must be acknowledged as being polysemous, having multi-layered meaning, capable of mediating many messages to its readers.'[6] This openness of meaning in Scripture is not, however, to be a kind of surrender to fanciful and idiosyncratic interpretation. In the development of further understandings, 'The process is not one of wilful imposition but of sympathetic exploration.'[7] What comes to light is what was always latently present. A Christian theologian will express this by saying that the same Spirit who inspired Scripture is also its interpreter within the developing understanding of the community of the Church.[8] While there are obviously variations in spiritual power and relevance between books of the Bible (no one supposes Jonah to be as significant as John), the modern canonical emphasis on trying to take Scripture as a whole is a necessary part of our engagement with it. 'Only then [will] the untidiness yet hopefulness of life find its match in the untidiness yet hopefulness of scripture.'[9]

Peacocke tells us that, 'The faith of the Christian church derives from its experience, the principal resource and source for which are those archetypal and seminal experiences and encounters with God recorded in its scriptures.'[10] He relies largely on a report of the Church of England Doctrine Commission[11] for an account of how the riches of this resource are to be made our own. There is an emphasis on 'fluidity of interpretation' and 'a subtle, varied and complex' relation of narrative to history.[12] Barbour, for his part, espouses the insights of narrative theology, with its emphasis on the role of story.[13] I would want to suggest that there is an important distinction between the power of story and the further power of true story. Even quite a simple narrative – say, of rescue from a burning building – can move us deeply when we know that it actually happened. The great impact of Thomas Keneally's novel *Schindler's Ark* derives not just from the skill of the narration, but also from the fact that there really was an Oscar Schindler who, despite his raffish life, showed great generosity and bravery in rescuing Polish Jews from death in the Nazi concentration camps.

Barbour is right to state, 'The biblical stories of creation, covenant, and Christ differ greatly in their historicity.'[14] The first is a symbolic expression of theological truth; the second is a much reworked account of a deliverance from past slavery and a commitment to the God who delivers; the third is an interpreted account of a life lived in first-century Palestine: '*Jesus of Nazareth* was a historical person, and we have more historical information about him than we do about Moses. But in calling him Christ and in testifying to his redemptive role we are making statements of faith that are not historically provable, though they are related to historical evidence.'[15] Barbour does not go on to give an account of what he believes we actually know historically about Jesus.

Peacocke and I, on the other hand, do address this question.[16] We both acknowledge the problems faced by those of us who cannot claim to be New Testament experts, but the matter is simply too important to be left to them alone, and in any case they are far from presenting an agreed assessment. We have to do the best we can. 'When the experts disagree, which is very often on detailed exegesis, one can but take note and rely on the kind of common sense we employ when we make those judgements which determine our personal actions.'[17] 'While I respect and value the insights that scholars provide, I cannot believe the matter should be left solely in their hands. ... The first question, surely, is whether the Gospels give the impression of having behind them a powerful personality whose character we can at least partially discern. I believe the answer to be yes.'[18] Like Peacocke, I incline to 'an *a priori* more "trusting" attitude to the scriptures',[19] though neither of us wishes to be credulous.

I have attempted to give a fairly detailed analysis of what we may know about Jesus. Peacocke gives a briefer sketch. We both have to discuss the question of miracles[20] for, to say the least, tales of Jesus' healings are woven into the Gospel accounts in such a way that they cannot naturally be excised. We agree that the central question is that of the coherence and consistency of divine action. 'A theologically acceptable account of miracles will have to incorporate them within a total, and totally consistent, understanding of God's activity, and not see them as singular exceptions.'[21] Yet consistency is not the same as dreary uniformity: 'It is conceivable that unexpected events occur in unprecedented circumstances.'[22] The central Christian miracle is the resurrection; I will return to that later.

Concern with what can be known historically about Jesus stems from the central role he plays in Christian thought. The very label 'Christian' conveys the assumption that a particular degree of significance is being assigned to Jesus Christ. Yet there are many and various ways in which this has been understood and experienced. An excellent method of exploring the manner in which the scientist-theologians approach matters of particularity is to consider their different Christologies.[23] In addition, one should also consider their approaches to the resurrection and to the virginal conception. In this way, one can gain considerable insight into how each one believes that Christian theology can be done in a scientific age.

Barbour's thinking is woven around two concepts: relationship and history. He rejects patristic talk of natures and substance, saying instead, 'What was unique about Christ, in other words, was his relationship to God, not his metaphysical "substance".'[24] Those theologians, like Geoffrey Lampe, who speak of the divine Spirit as inspiring Jesus to an unparalleled degree, were, in Barbour's opinion, on the right track. In consequence, he suggests 'that in comparing Christ and other people, as in comparing human and nonhuman life, we should speak of *differences in degree*. These can add up to differences in kind, but with no absolute lines.'[25] (Not all will find the comparison compelling – after all, there seems a rather remarkable distinction between self-conscious, moral human beings and, at most, conscious, amoral animal beings.) The idea of Christ as being, so to speak, outstandingly human, can for Barbour find historical expression in evolutionary terms: 'I suggest then, that in an *evolutionary perspective* we may view both the human and divine activity in Christ as a continuation and intensification of what had been occurring previously. We can think of him as representing a new stage in evolution and a new stage in God's activity.'[26] Clearly, Barbour is attributing a prime significance to Jesus, but in a way that will cause no shock or disturbance to a scientific mind, accustomed to think of new emergents in evolutionary terms. The question is whether this somewhat bland Christology is adequate to the strangeness and hopefulness of Christian experience. I shall suggest that it is not.

Many of the same themes surface also in Peacocke. Reflection on evolutionary history 'encourages us to understand the "incarnation" which occurred in Jesus as exemplifying that emergence-from-continuity which characterizes the whole process whereby God is creating continuously through discontinuity'.[27] Thus in Christ we see 'the distinctive manifestation of a possibility always inherently there for human beings in their potential nature ... what we have affirmed about Jesus is not, in principle, impossible for all humanity'.[28] The role of Christ seems to be presented as being both the exemplar of possibility and the exhibitor of information about God. 'Might it not be possible for a human being so to reflect God, to be so wholly open to God, that God's presence was clearly unveiled to the rest of humanity in a new, emergent and unexpected manner?'[29] I have criticized Christological thought that relies too much on the 'window into God' account as being a kind of revived gnosticism. Its emphasis is on divine communication through the man Jesus:

> No account of the incarnation will fail to emphasize that Jesus makes God known to us in the plainest possible terms, by living the life of a man, but to rely on the revelatory character of his life alone is to adopt a gnostic account of our redemption. Let me say again that I believe our need is for transformation, not just information.[30]

In contrast, Peacocke takes a strong view of revelatory communication with men and women as being God's mode of action with humanity.[31]

Christologies of an inspirational and functional kind, such as

I have been describing, by no means deny that God acted in a special way through Christ. However, the particular character of the event is held to be, as Barbour says, a matter of degree and to lie in an intensification of the activity of the divine Spirit in a human life. Evolutionary language is quite appropriate to such an understanding, because the incarnation is seen as a culmination of God's continuing action in creation. The critical question is whether this is adequate to Christian experience or whether the latter demands divine presence rather than divine inspiration, participation rather than communication, so that the incarnation must be expressed in ontological rather than functional terms. However mysterious and difficult to articulate the former understanding may be, it seems to me that an indispensable Christian insight is that in Christ the Creator actually shared in the travail of his creation.

In fact, this is a theme that is also present in what Peacocke has to say. This more orthodox Christology, which sees God as fully present in Christ and not simply inspiring or informing him, can go on to interpret the suffering of the cross as God's actual participation in the bitterness of this world. It is a powerful insight, meeting the perplexities of suffering at the deepest possible level.[32] Peacocke recognizes this: 'But if God were present in and one with Jesus the Christ, then we have to conclude that *God* also suffered in and with him in his passion and death.'[33] There seems to me to be an unreconciled discrepancy between this insight and an inspirational theory of the nature of Christ. Peacocke's evolutionary account of Christology does not appear to offer the degree of identification between God and Christ that this crucial insight of theodicy demands. A similar criticism applies to his account of the atonement.[34] We can only say, as we both want to say, that we see 'in the life, suffering and death of Jesus the Christ, in his humanly experienced anguish, *God* going to the ultimate in suffering love on behalf of humanity, an act of Love "for us"',[35] if God actually *was* 'in Christ, reconciling the world to himself' (2 Cor. 5.19). However shocking it may be to the secular scientific mind, I believe that Christian theology can only make sense of its experience on the basis of a strong account of the incarnation. That is not to say, of course, that this account must be expressed in the categories of Hellenist thought of the fourth and fifth centuries. We have to struggle to make this fundamental insight our own in the *theological* terms available to us today.

Such a strong account is what I have sought to explore and defend in my own writing. So mysterious a belief calls for adequate motivation. I start the discussion with the writers of the New Testament,[36] where 'the dominant impression is of people groping for concepts capable of doing justice to their experience'.[37] These monotheistic Jews use strange formulae, like Paul's oft-repeated greeting 'Grace to you and peace from God our Father and the Lord Jesus Christ'. God and Christ are bracketed together, and the divine attribute of Lordship is accorded to Jesus, because that seemed demanded by the character of the Church's encounter with its risen Lord. Yet how this was to be understood required further theological reflection.

The first Christological theory we can detect was adoptionism, the idea that the man Jesus was found worthy of exaltation to divine status.[38] It was soon abandoned because the Church felt it had to accord divine initiative to the 'Christ-event', from start to finish. 'The exaltation of Jesus could not be pictured as a piece of divine opportunism, trading in the fortunate occurrence of a man worthy of resurrection. God must have been at work in Jesus throughout.'[39] This led to concepts of pre-existence (see John 1, Col. 1, Heb. 1, and, some think, the pre-Pauline hymn of Phil. 2.6-11). Struggle with these mysterious ideas continued for centuries, leading to, but not ending at, the Council of Chalcedon in the year 451. It is important that early Christian thinking on the natures of Christ arose in the context of a struggle with experience, and not as the result of some unbridled metaphysical speculation. All the scientist-theologians are concerned with a Christology 'from below', building on the evidence. I believe that a strong incarnational Christology is the best attempt to make sense of the data of Jesus' life and death and resurrection, and the Church's experience of him.

A theological way of expressing this 'bottom-up' thinker's emphasis on experience is to say that it is the work of Christ that is the key to the nature of Christ.[40] The fundamental Christian experience, from New Testament times onwards, has been that in Christ there is the transforming power of a new life in which we are able to share. No account of him that is not able to explain how this can be so will satisfy theological thinking. I believe that:

> The saving work of Christ and his corporate character are attested by Christian experience and, in my view, enforce necessary conditions which any adequate Christology must succeed in meeting. I think that evolutionary Christologies, which speak of Jesus as the 'new emergent', signally fail to pass this test.[41]

If Jesus has 'emerged', how can that avail for us? It will not be enough simply to appeal to his true humanity and 'conjecture that what happened in and to him could happen in and to us'.[42] Peacocke in fact recognizes that there must be a divine initiative involved. In his discussion of the work of Christ,[43] he eventually settles for what one might call a neo-Abelardian account of atonement, 'seeing the life, suffering and death of Jesus the Christ as an *act of love* ... an act of love *of God*'.[44] It seems to me that this insight is part of the truth but, once again, for it to be true we require a strong concept of the incarnation. Peacocke goes on to say:

> Recognition of the continuity of Jesus the Christ with ourselves has already enabled us to see him as the forerunner, the first realization and instantiation of, a new possibility for human existence. We perceive in him that this is not a mere possibility but can actually be the case in a human response of costly obedience and of openness to God which was itself an initiative of God in his outreach to humanity – that is, God as Holy Spirit, immanent within the created world.[45]

The last clause just saves the remark from a tendency that I have otherwise detected and criticized in Peacocke, of inclining towards 'a kind of Pelagian Christology'.[46]

My own belief is that the work of Christ is only made intelligible if there was present in his full humanity also the life of full divinity, so that he constitutes the ontological link between human need and divine saving power.[47] If sin is separation from God, salvation is a restored sharing in the divine life. 'God alone can redeem us from the entail of sin and the flawed life which results from our alienation from him. Only divine action can save us, and the agent must really be there in the event.'[48] Salvation is made accessible to us because there is the possibility of a human solidarity in Christ, a sharing in his risen life, expressed for example in the Pauline language that the Church is the body of Christ (1 Cor. 12.27). 'I do not think that we can make full sense of the Christian understanding of Christ's death without being prepared to embrace the notion of a degree of human solidarity, a notion so foreign to our individualistic, atomized, Western thinking, though it would not be strange, I suspect, to someone from tribal Africa.'[49]

Divine and human natures in one person, and the coinherence of humanity in Christ, are mysterious ideas, uncongenial to the secular twentieth-century mind. They have arisen in Christian thinking, not from an obscurantist urge to mystify, nor from a fanciful propensity to speculation, but from the struggle to do justice to actual Christian experience. They represent ideas that have to be struggled with precisely because of their theological indispensability. I do not think these concepts can be abandoned in accommodation to the supposed needs of a scientific age. Theology has its own necessary concepts, just as quantum physics has its own necessary concepts. Neither can submit to being reduced to the banalities of common sense. After all, 'A scientist expects a fundamental theory to be tough, surprising and exciting.'[50]

These epithets apply especially to the central Christian assertion of the resurrection of Christ. What could be more counterintuitive than that a man should come alive again, nevermore to die? Yet *something* happened to turn the demoralized disciples of Good Friday into the confident proclaimers of Pentecost. Jesus' life ended in apparent total failure:

'It seems to me entirely possible that if Jesus had not been raised from the dead we would never have heard of him.'[51] No one writing from a Christian perspective can fail to say something about what they might understand by Christ's resurrection.

Barbour mentions the resurrection from time to time, but he does not give it extended attention or develop his thoughts about it to any great degree. He tells us, 'Process theology directs attention to Christ's life and the suffering of the cross, and it sees the resurrection as evidence of the transforming power of that love rather than as an independent manifestation of God's power.'[52] It is not clear what is the nature of the 'evidence' being referred to. The cross by itself is so ambiguous an event that it is certainly not self-interpreting in isolation.[53] As to 'independent manifestation of God's power', it is hard to see how such a concept could relate satisfactorily to the largely spectatorial and persuasive God of process thought.[54]

Peacocke considers the resurrection at greater length.[55] He relies quite heavily on the writing of the American New Testament scholar, Pheme Perkins. His discussion begins with psychological reflections on the appearance tradition. The willingness of disciples to die for their faith suggests that the probability of a merely hallucinatory explanation is 'minimal':

> The evidence is, therefore, that this was a genuine psychological experience, that is, within the consciousness of these witnesses. Note that this does not necessarily imply that they were 'merely' psychological, with no reference to reality, if they can be shown to form part of a meaningful pattern that requires a higher-level autonomous theory to make it intelligible.... This concept of 'resurrection' need not be reducible to any purely psychological account and the affirmations of the New Testament that propose this concept can properly be claimed to be referring to a new kind of reality hitherto unknown because not hitherto experienced.[56]

In other words, there can be more to resurrection than psychology, provided that 'more' makes theological sense. Peacocke's discussion of what that 'more' might be is cautious and hedged. He takes seriously the general testimony of the New Testament to the resurrection:.

> The historical evidence for the disciples experiencing a manifestation of the person of Jesus after his death, in the terms in which we have described it, is indeed strong. Yet the complex of experiences were of such a kind that one hesitates to describe the resurrection as a 'miracle' in the sense of an 'intervention' by God *in* the natural order of events since its end-result was not a clearly defined natural state.[57]

In the latter sentence, Peacocke appears simply to be rejecting the idea that Jesus was resuscitated, a proposal that no serious theologian has ever entertained.[58] He seems happier with the exaltation language of the Epistle to the Hebrews than with the resurrection language which is more characteristic of the rest of the New Testament. The conclusion Peacocke reaches can be summarized in the following words:

> The resurrection of Jesus is perhaps better described as an experience of the disciples which they could interpret only as a disclosure by God that the human being of Jesus existed after his death in an entirely new mode, or level. Such a disclosure would have involved transformation/re-creation of the dead Jesus to which the regularities and 'laws' of the natural sciences and ordinary experience do not in principle apply.[59]

In the course of his discussion, Peacocke tells us, 'The evidence that the tomb was empty is not as strong as that for the resurrection appearances to the disciples',[60] and he therefore presents us with two options: either the transformation of Jesus' dead body or an agnosticism about its actual fate. The statement about the evidence for the empty tomb is one that is frequently made but it is open to reassessment.[61] It depends principally upon Paul's not having referred to the empty tomb, and in particular an absence of reference to it in the earliest account we have of the appearances, the brief list of 1 Corinthians 15.3–8. Yet that spare account makes mention that Jesus 'was buried'. This has suggested to some of us that Paul knew that there was a special significance in the tomb of Jesus, and that, as a first-century Jew, he could not have believed that Jesus lived if his body was known to be still mouldering in the grave. Certainly, the opponents of Christianity, from the first century onwards, seem always to have accepted that there was a tomb that was found empty, but they sought to explain it away by such implausible suggestions as that the disciples had stolen the body. It is striking that all four Gospels give essentially the same account of the women finding the tomb empty, while their descriptions of the appearances are puzzlingly diverse. Furthermore, if the tale were concocted, then why, in the male-dominated ancient world, were women assigned the leading role?

My own approach to the resurrection[62] begins with a survey of the New Testament evidence, and I have already sketched some considerations relating to the empty tomb. I must confess to some perplexity at the variety of the Gospel stories of the appearances, with their diverse emphases on Jerusalem or Galilee as the locality. Yet:

> Amid the variety of the appearance stories there is one element which is both unexpected and persistent. It is that there was difficulty in recognizing the risen Jesus.... This would be a strange motif to recur in stories which were merely made up. It seems likely to me that, on the contrary, it is the kernel of a genuine historical reminiscence.[63]

In addition to these motivations for belief arising from the New Testament, there are certain other considerations of a more general character. Why did the first, Sabbath-observing, Jewish Christians designate the first day of the week as the Lord's day, if it were not for the fact that they regarded it as the day of resurrection? Then there is the characteristic testimony of the Church down the centuries, which always speaks of Jesus as the living Lord of the present and not as the revered Founder of the past. I concluded my survey of the evidence by saying:

> I hope I have made it clear that there is motivation for the belief that Jesus was raised from the dead (the most ancient

expression is always in the passive; it is a great act of God, not a final miracle of Jesus, which is being asserted). We now have to ask the question whether the motivation provided is in fact strong enough to support the extraordinary claim being made. ... Can it make sense within a general understanding of God and his ways with humanity that, alone of all who have ever lived, this man was restored to unending life in an act which, although it transcends history, nevertheless is embedded in history?[64]

We return to the inescapable question associated with any claim for miracle: does it correspond to a coherent and consistent understanding of divine action? I believe that the resurrection of Jesus makes sense in this way because it fulfils three conditions: (i) it was not fitting that his life should end in total failure; (ii) it was not fitting that God should abandon the one man who wholly put his trust in him; (iii) it is fitting that our deep hopes that death does not have the last word about human significance should be vindicated.

It is important to recognize that in Christian thought, the singularity of Jesus' resurrection lies in its timing and not in its occurrence. He anticipates within history a destiny that awaits all other humankind beyond history. 'For as in Adam all die, so also in Christ shall all be made alive' (1 Cor. 15.21). Moreover, the significance of the empty tomb's message that the Lord's glorified body is the transmutation of his dead body, is that in Christ there is a destiny for *matter* as well as humankind. Jesus' resurrection is the seed from which God's new creation has begun to grow. Peacocke rightly expresses this hope also when he says that the resurrection could be seen 'as a sign of the ultimate destiny not only of human beings, but of the whole created order in the eternal purposes of God'.[65] Unfortunately he goes on to question this, because he regards it as problematic what will happen to us because the atoms of our corpses will disperse with time. It is difficult to see where the problem lies, since we all recognize that there is nothing specifically significant about those individual atoms. After all, they are changing all the while in the course of our lives. It is the pattern that is me that will be re-created by God in the new environment brought about by his eschatological act of general resurrection.[66] We shall be resurrected, not reassembled.

Ultimately all hope of resurrection, for Jesus in history or for ourselves beyond history, depends on the eternal faithfulness of God (see Mark 12.26–7). He alone is the one whose loving purposes will not be frustrated by transience and death.

The conclusion I reach can be summarized in the words:

> the only explanation which is commensurate with the phenomena is that Jesus rose from the dead in such a fashion (whatever that may be) that it is true to say that he is alive today, glorified and exalted but still continuously related in a mysterious but real way with the historical figure who lived and died in first-century Palestine.[67]

Comparison with Peacocke's conclusion (p. 75) shows that, though we have travelled rather different paths, we have arrived at somewhat similar destinations.

The final example of particularity I want to consider is the virgin birth or, more strictly, the virginal conception. It is far less a matter of concern in the New Testament than is the resurrection. The latter is mentioned in practically every book and the New Testament writings would be incomprehensible if all references to it were excised. The virginal conception, however, is only clearly referred to in the well-known birth narratives of Matthew and Luke (not immediately easily reconcilable with each other) and possibly a few stray hints elsewhere.[68] In terms of motivating evidence, the case is thin. It is scarcely surprising that so many theologians find the idea difficult, or wish to be agnostic about it. Yet I think it presents an interesting test case for how one weighs theological arguments in reaching one's conclusions.

Unsurprisingly, Barbour, as far as I am aware, does not refer at all to the virginal conception. Peacocke, on the other hand, gives it quite an extensive discussion.[69] He concentrates on genetics, explaining that in order to be male Jesus needed XY chromosomes, that Mary could only supply an X, and so at least his Y chromosome must have been miraculously provided.

At one level, this is simply the modern way of expressing an ancient thought, that virginal conception is contrary to nature and could only be brought about by divine action. At a deeper level, Peacocke feels that such a divine provision of genetic information would prejudice Jesus' true humanity. 'In the light of our biological knowledge it is then impossible to see how Jesus could be said to share our human nature if he came into existence by a virginal conception of the kind traditionally proposed.'[70] If that were correct, it would be a very strong theological argument against the virginal conception, since it is central to orthodox Christian understanding that Jesus was truly and fully human. If he did not share our nature, he could not be our saviour. Yet I am not convinced that the argument is sound. The dual origin of the X and Y chromosomes (if that is what was involved) seems a possible physical expression of the belief, in the words of the Nicene creed, that Jesus 'by the power of the Holy Spirit became incarnate of the Virgin Mary and was made man'. In other words, his conception was an act of divine–human co-operation.

My own consideration of the question begins with the recognition that the story of the virginal conception has been widely seen as a way of expressing the fusion of divine initiative and human response in the inauguration of the life of Jesus, in which the power of the divine Spirit and the human obedience of Mary both play their parts. The question is whether this is just a symbolic tale or an historically enacted event. Because I believe it is the essence of Christianity to combine the mythical and the historical (p. 65), I concluded that 'the words "born of the Virgin Mary" can be a proper part of the creed of a bottom-up thinker'.[71] The scriptural evidence by itself would scarcely be enough; considerations of theological appropriateness must be given great weight if we are to accept the virginal conception.

The scientist-theologians all recognize that their Christian faith involves them in an engagement with particularity, and especially with the particularity of Jesus Christ, and they all recognize that God was at work in him in a special way. The manner in which they make this engagement and describe this divine involvement in Christ differs, and in these differences we can see most clearly the divergencies of their theological methods and understandings. In relation to the motivating evidence for Christian belief, there is a spectrum running from reliance on rather general considerations of Christian experience, sympathetically and carefully considered, to an attitude that requires as part of its investigation a scrupulous assessment of detailed parts of the New Testament testimony. In relation to the interpretative categories brought to bear in the quest for theological understanding, there is a spectrum running from the use of concepts that sit rather easily with contemporary culture and scientific ways of thought to an attitude that recognizes that theology must employ its own concepts, however strange and counterintuitive they may seem to twentieth-century secular thinking. In both these spectra, Barbour is towards one end; I am towards the other; and Peacocke is somewhere in between us.

7

Consonance or Assimilation?

THE SCIENTIST-THEOLOGIANS have much in common as they seek to take science seriously within their shared heritage of the Christian tradition. Yet the foregoing discussion will also have made it clear that there are distinct and significant differences of method and conclusion among us. None of us wants a compartmentalized account, in which science and theology are insulated from each other because they are supposed to operate in disjoint realms. We all recognize that the two disciplines influence each other and that there is intellectual traffic traversing the open border between them. The ultimate unity of our knowledge of the one world of human experience is affirmed by us all.

The critical question is the degree of autonomy that each discipline must claim, both in maintaining the validity of the experience of reality to which it has particular access, and also in the generation of its own particular concepts that are required to give an adequate and insightful account of that experience. None of us wishes to assert a takeover of religion by science, so that the former becomes just an emotional or motivational gloss on the latter. Absorption of religion by science is not on any of our agendas. We all defend the thesis that religion rightly makes cognitive claims of novel kinds. Equally, we all acknowledge that modern discoveries about the nature and history of the physical world have had the effect of modifying in various respects the tone of theological discourse.

We are all, to some extent, revisionists. The question at issue is the degree to which that revision should seek to contain itself within an intellectual trajectory in continuity with the insights and affirmations of the always-developing tradition of the Christian Church. We would all agree that the answer to that question is to be determined by the overriding condition of conformity to the truth, but we differ in our conclusions about what this implies for contemporary Christian thinking. A simple illustration is provided by the discussion of Christology in Chapter 6. Barbour, Peacocke and I all wish to assign a prime significance to Jesus Christ, but we differ significantly in our understandings of what is an adequate and intelligible way of doing so in the twentieth century. Are evolutionary and developmental ideas, so accessible and congenial to our contemporaries, the means fortunately available for us to fulfil this task, with Jesus playing the role of a 'new emergent', or does an account that does justice to the Christian experience of new life in Christ still demand for its adequate articulation some re-appropriation of the deeply mysterious and exciting idea of the incarnation as classically understood? Is a functional Christology sufficient (in which the difference in the case of Christ resides in the measure of his openness to God and his degree of inspiration by the Spirit), or do we need an ontological Christology (in which the life of Christ is understood as being the unequivocal participation of the Creator in the life of creation)?

At issue is the degree to which scientific concepts should be allowed to mould and influence the conceptual apparatus of theological thought, and the degree to which theology must retain (as science does unquestioned) its own portfolio of irreducibly necessary ideas. At one end of the spectrum is assimilation, the effort to blend scientific and theological categories to the maximum possible extent without succumbing to the surrender of absorption, so as to produce a religious understanding that will place the minimum strain on secular thinking, that will provide the most accessible presentation of Christian belief, and that will afford the most obvious way of integrating human knowledge. There is no denying that there is some attractiveness about this approach. At the other end of the spectrum is consonance, which acknowledges that scientific discoveries constrain modes of theological expression, so that they have to be consistent with the truth of what we know about the physical world, but which also claims that, because the reality that theology seeks to encounter and apprehend must be known in ways that conform to the divine nature, it is an endeavour that (to the extent to which deity is describable by finite human minds) requires the use of analogies stretched in novel ways and the use of unparalleled concepts arising from the way in which God has in fact chosen to act and to make himself known. In my opinion, there is no denying to theology this degree of proper autonomy, analogous to the autonomy in its own domain that science enjoys as of right.

None of the scientist-theologians represents a pure case of the extremes of this classification. It seems to me that Barbour is located towards the assimilation end of the spectrum. While there is an unmistakably Christian tone to his writing, he does not often engage with the detailed substance of traditional Christian theology. It may seem a trifle ironic that his preferred metaphysical framework for discussion is that provided by process philosophy, since I feel that Whitehead's thought is inadequately anchored in our actual knowledge of physical process (p. 28).

I place myself very much towards the consonance end of the spectrum. Christian theology must adapt its thinking to modern scientific ideas, where these impinge on its understanding of what is going on in creation. The doctrine of the Fall certainly needs radical reconsideration.[1] An Augustinian notion of decay from an original paradisal state, brought about by a single disastrous ancestral act, is one that cannot be made consonant with what we know about the history of the Earth. Following principles that St Augustine himself enunciated, it is therefore necessary to reconsider what the meaning of this biblical story may be. Another particularly significant example of the need for further thought can be identified in relation to eschatology and ultimate hope. The universe as we presently know it is condemned to eventual futility. Yet if there is an assurance of fulfilment beyond this dismal ending, it must rest in the possibility of a transforming new act by the ever-faithful Creator. I have sought to defend in contemporary terms the credibility of such a hope.[2]

Despite the need for engagement with contemporary thought, I think that theologically we also need to benefit from the insights of preceding generations: 'The theologian of the twentieth century enjoys no presumptive superiority over the theologians of the fourth or sixteenth centuries. Indeed, those earlier centuries may well have had access to spiritual experiences and insights which have been attenuated, or even lost, in our time.'[3]

I find it more difficult to know where to place Peacocke in the spectrum. At times he appears to me to operate in an assimilationist mode and at other times in a consonantist mode (see the discussion of Christology, pp. 69–70).

It might seem natural to label the assimilation/consonance dichotomy as being an aspect of the liberal/conservative divide. However, I think this would be a mistake. My consonantist stance does not derive simply from a desire to hang on to the past; if radical revision actually proved to be necessary, the consequences would have to be accepted. Barbour's assimilationist stance, I am sure, is not driven by an undue desire to conform to the spirit of the age. We are all trying, in our separate ways, to find the truth. The differences arise from different understandings of how theology relates to general culture and where the balance of mutual influence is to be found. We none of us approach these questions with the answers prejudged, but we do not agree in our assessments of when traditional concepts have to give way to a mode of contemporary thinking that is motivated from outside theology itself.

Two distinguished theologians of the twentieth century, Richard Niebuhr[4] and Hans Frei,[5] have discussed the general issue of how theology may be related to its inescapable cultural setting, and they have presented us with suggested typologies of differing solutions to this problem.

Niebuhr takes a very wide view of the nature of culture; it refers as much to manners and experience as it does to perception and belief. Science can only be one small component of such a cultural setting. Niebuhr's discussion is subtle and nuanced, at times making distinctions that are very fine and not altogether easy to discern with confidence. A crude summary can do little justice to the perceptive complexity of his argument about the various ways in which Christ and culture can be related. In broad terms, we are presented with five possibilities: (1) Christ against culture (the theological judgement of the inadequacy of secular culture); (2) the Christ of culture (theology comfortably at home within culture); (3) Christ above culture (a synthesis of a 'both-and' kind); (4) Christ and culture in paradox (a dialectical tension between the theological and the secular); (5) Christ the transformer of culture (the eventual conversion of culture). It would seem that assimilationists will largely be associated with type (2) and consonantists will largely be associated with either (3) or (5). Yet we should note that in relation to the question of how Christian life relates to society, Barbour has classified himself as type (5).[6]

Frei sets out, in a work unfortunately not completed before his death, to explore the question of whether theology is to be regarded as a part of *Wissenschaft* (wide human knowledge) or whether it is to be regarded as religion-specific. He notes that these possibilities are not necessarily mutually exclusive, but some balance may be struck between them. He too finds five types, and again the discussion is too subtle for satisfactory summary. Yet one may identify, in a broad-brush way, five possibilities: (1) theology as philosophy and so part of the academy; (2) theology as an academic discipline, but with a distinctive Christian character; (3) theology and culture correlated with each other in ad hoc and relatively even-handed ways, but with no covering 'super-theory'; (4) a correlation in which 'the practical discipline of Christian self-description governs and limits the applicability of general criteria of meaning in theology, rather than vice versa';[7] (5) theology as an exclusively Christian discipline. Barbour's style of Christian thought in an easy and accommodating relationship with scientific culture would seem to place him in type (2). Peacocke's metaphysical reticence and his mixed thoughts about Christology seem naturally associated with type (3). My own insistence on the autonomy of theology in its dialogue with scientific culture would seem to make type (4) my appropriate assignment. Frei emphasizes that these are all possible ways of doing theology (he cites examples of distinguished practitioners of each type), and while one can detect certain preferences in his thinking, he does not compose an order of merit.

We can essay a similar generosity of assessment in relation to the more modest and limited exploration of the conduct of the science and theology debate. Naturally, I prefer the strategy of consonance, which seems to me to hold out the best prospect of doing equal justice to modern knowledge and past insight, but I greatly benefit from the writings of my colleagues, with whom I share the common cause of the pursuit of truth.

There is one final thing to say. Those who engage in interdisciplinary work cannot avoid taking intellectual risks as they venture beyond the safe perimeter of their primary discipline. I cannot claim an expert knowledge extending beyond fundamental physics, so that in the rest of science, and on into philosophy and theology, I cannot pretend to be more than someone who takes a serious interest in the issues involved but who has not been able to devote a lifetime to study of them. I do not think that means that I am deprived of any right to reach conclusions on these wider matters, for none of us is condemned to the prisonhouse of our narrow speciality – since we are human beings before we are experts. We must seek to listen to the experts but we cannot simply capitulate to them – particularly when they do not speak with one voice.

One reason why I have made extensive use of quotations from other authors in most of my writings (which are of a somewhat different character from the present comparative study) is that I wish to show that the positions I espouse are not without support in the relevant professional community. Needless to say, the diverse multi-tongued discourse of philosophy and theology means that no one could look for more than some degree of support, whatever point of view they adopted!

I think that similar considerations apply to my scientist-theologian colleagues. This implies that our contributions to the science and theology debate, though we believe them to be of value, cannot possibly exhaust the content of that debate. I would like to see more theologians, not just taking an occasional interest in these matters, but joining in a more sustained way in the interdisciplinary encounter. There is much work still to be done, and we need their help.

NOTES

1 *INTRODUCTION*

1 B. Davies, *The Thought of Thomas Aquinas* (Oxford University Press, 1992).

2 For a survey of twentieth-century philosophy of science, see W. H. Newton-Smith, *The Rationality of Science* (Routledge & Kegan Paul, 1981); for various views on scientific realism, see J. Leplin (ed.), *Scientific Realism* (University of California Press, 1984); for my own defence of realism in relation to elementary particle physics, see J. C. Polkinghorne, *Rochester Roundabout* (Longman, 1989), ch. 21. I shall not argue the point further here, but all the scientist-theologians take the view that science affords us a verisimilitudinous account of the pattern and history of the physical world.

3 For a robust criticism of scientism, see M. Midgley, *Evolution as Religion* (Methuen, 1985).

4 See M. Polanyi, *Personal Knowledge* (Routledge & Kegan Paul, 1958).

5 L. Gilkey, *Nature, Reality and the Sacred* (Augsburg Fortress, 1993), p. 39.

6 T. F. Torrance, *Theological Science* (Oxford University Press, 1969); I. G. Barbour, *Myths, Models and Paradigms* (SCM Press, 1974) (referred to as *MMP*); A. R. Peacocke, *Intimations of Reality* (University of Notre Dame Press, 1984) (referred to as *IR*); J. C. Polkinghorne, *Reason and Reality* (SPCK, 1991) (referred to as *RR*).

7 I. G. Barbour, *Issues in Science and Religion* (SCM Press, 1966); *Religion in an Age of Science* (SCM Press, 1990) (referred to as *RAS*). Many of the issues discussed in *RAS* were first addressed in the earlier book.

8 A. R. Peacocke, *Creation and the World of Science* (Oxford University Press, 1979) (referred to as *CWS*); *God and the New Biology* (Dent, 1986) (referred to as *GNB*); *Theology for a Scientific Age* (enlarged edn, SCM Press, 1993) (referred to as *TSA*).

9 J. C. Polkinghorne, *One World* (SPCK, 1986); *Science and Creation* (SPCK, 1988) (referred to as *SC*); *Science and Providence* (SPCK, 1989) (referred to as *SP*); *Science and Christian Belief* (SPCK, 1994; also published as *The Faith of a Physicist*, Princeton University Press, 1994) (referred to as *SCB*).

10 *RAS*, ch. 1.

11 *RR*, ch. 6.

12 This has by no means been confined to those with conventional theological interests. See P. W. Davies, *God and the New Physics* (Dent, 1983); *The Mind of God* (Simon & Schuster, 1992); and in a different way, J. D. Barrow and F. J. Tipler, *The Anthropic Cosmological Principle (Oxford University Press,* 1986); J. Leslie, *Universes* (Routledge, 1989).

13 For example, *CWS*, chs 2–5; P. Teilhard de Chardin, *The Phenomenon of Man* (Collins, 1959).

14 An early use of this concept was made by E. McMullin in A. R. Peacocke (ed.), *The Sciences and Theology in the Twentieth Century* (Oriel Press, 1981), pp. 17–57.

15 See Barbour: *RAS*, chs 8 and 9; Peacocke: *IR*, ch. 2; *TSA*, ch. 9; Polkinghorne: *SP*; *RR*, ch. 3; *SCB*, pp. 67–9, 77–82.

16 In my view, such a facile connection through verbal parallels characterizes the attempted assimilation of Eastern mysticism to quantum physics in F. Capra, *The Tao of Physics* (Wildwood House, 1975).

17 *SCB*, ch. 7.

18 W. Pannenberg, *Towards a Theology of Nature* (ed. T. Peters), (Westminster/John Knox Press, 1993). For a critique, see *RR*, pp. 92–4.

19 Barbour: *RAS*; Peacocke: *TSA*; Polkinghorne: *SCB*; all are Gifford lectures.

20 *SCB*, p. 7.

2 *MOTIVATED BELIEF: CRITICAL REALISM*

1 *RAS*, p. 16.

2 *IR*, p. 51.

3 *SCB*, pp. 46–7.

4 *SCB*, p. 70.

5 J. C. Polkinghorne, *Beyond Science* (Cambridge University Press, 1996), ch. 8.

6 *RAS*, p. 267.

7 *RAS*, pp. 64–5.

8 *TSA*, p. 136.

9 *TSA*, p. 339.

10 *RR*, pp. 18–19.

11 *SC*, p. 86.

12 N. Murphy, *Theology in the Age of Scientific Reasoning* (Cornell University Press, 1990), p. 196.

13 Barbour: *MMP*, pp. 34–8; *RAS*, pp. 31–47; Peacocke: *IR*, ch. 1; *TSA*, pp. 11–19; Polkinghorne: *RR*, ch. 1; *SCB*, ch. 2.

14 *RAS* p. 44.

15 IR, p. 25.

16 See Polkinghorne, *Rochester Roundabout.*

17 *SC*, p. 32; *RR*, p. 11; cf. *CWS*, pp. 33–8.

18 J. C. Polkinghorne, *The Quantum World* (Longman, 1984), ch. 8. For a nuanced discussion of the veiled reality of the quantum world, see B. d'Espagnat, *Reality and the Physicist* (Cambridge University Press, 1989).

19 *SCB*, pp. 32–3.

20 See Chapter 1.

21 *SCB*, pp. 7–8.

22 *IR*, pp. 33, 45.

23 Barbour: *MMP*, chs 3–5; *RAS*, pp. 47–65; Peacocke: *IR*, ch. 1; Polkinghorne: *RR*, ch.2.

24 See *RR*, pp. 20–3, for illustrations of different ways that models are used in physics.

25 *MMP*, p. 6.

26 *IR*, p. 30.

27 *TSA*, p. 87.

28 *MMP*, p. 14; see also pp. 42–5.

29 *RR*, pp. 31–4. For a convenient account of modern thinking on symbol, see F. W. Dillistone, *The Power of Symbols* (SCM Press, 1986).

30 *SCB*, ch. 7.
31 *MMP*, *passim.*
32 *MMP*, p. 49.
33 *IR*, p. 31.
34 *RR*, p. 28.
35 See Polkinghorne, *Quantum World*, ch. 5.
36 *RR*, pp. 25–8; see also *MMP*, ch. 5.
37 *MMP*, p. 78.
38 *TSA*, p. 18; cf. *RR*, chs 4 & 6.
39 *TSA*, p. viii, my italics.
40 *SCB*, pp. 1, 8.

3 *EMBODIED EXISTENCE: AGENCY*

1 *TSA*, p. 41.
2 *TSA*, p. 77; see also pp. 230–2, 248–54.
3 P. Berger, *A Rumour of Angels* (Penguin, 1970).
4 *SCB*, p. 14.
5 Barbour: *RAS*, chs 8 and 9; Peacocke: *IR*, ch. 2; *TSA*, ch. 9; Polkinghorne: *SP*; *RR*, ch. 3; *SCB*, pp. 67–9, 77–82. See also R. J. Russell, N. Murphy, and C. J. Isham (eds), *Quantum Cosmology and the Laws of Nature* (Vatican Observatory, 1993); R. J. Russell, N. Murphy and A. R. Peacocke (eds), *Chaos, Complexity and Self-Organization* (Vatican Observatory, 1995).
6 Barbour: *Issues*; *RAS*, chs 8 and 9.
7 A. N. Whitehead, *Process and Reality* (The Free Press, 1978); for process theology, see C. Hartshorne, *The Divine Relativity* (Yale University Press, 1948); J. B. Cobb and D. R. Griffin, *Process Theology* (Westminster Press, 1976).
8 *RAS*, p. 226.
9 *RAS*, p. 227.
10 *SCB*, pp. 22–3.
11 *RR*, ch. 7. (In *SCB*, pp. 23–4, I give a critique of David Bohm's different metaphysical proposals based on his particular interpretation of quantum theory.) Measurement involves the macroscopic irreversible registration of an aspect of a microscopic quantum state. It does not imply the necessary intervention of a conscious observer. Measurements have often taken place in the universe at times and places where no such observers were present.
12 In a private communication, Arthur Peacocke has suggested that it is an advantage to restrict speculation to specific issues, such as mind-body, communication between persons, and divine self-communication, rather than attempting a more general metaphysical account. This is because (a) there is no generally agreed metaphysical position available today; (b) a piecemeal approach, worked out in relation to specific issues, is a better way of tackling the question and places less constraint on theology. He concludes, 'So the absence of a presupposed *general* metaphysic in my work I regard as one of its strengths.' My problem with this is that it is difficult to assess the credibility of concepts such as top-down causality without, at least, a tentative general picture in which they might find a consistent place.

13 *SC*, ch. 5; *RR*, ch. 3; *SCB*, ch. 1.
14 T. Nagel, *The View from Nowhere* (Oxford University Press, 1986), p. 30.
15 *SCB*, pp. 12–13.
16 M. F. Wiles, *God's Action in the World* (SCM Press, 1986).
17 A. M. Farrer, *A Science of God?* (Geoffrey Bles, 1968), p. 76.
18 Barbour: *RAS*, pp. 257–8; Peacocke: *TSA*, p.136; Polkinghorne: *SP*, pp. 5–7; *SCB*, p. 82.
19 *SCB*, pp. 81–2.
20 *IR*, p. 63.
21 *TSA*, p. 149.
22 *RAS*, p. 181.
23 See the article by C. J. Isham and J. C. Polkinghorne in Russell *et al.*, *Quantum Cosmology*, pp. 135–44.
24 *TSA*, p. 371.
25 Hartshorne, *Divine Relativity*, p. 90.
26 *SP*, pp. 15–16; *SCB*, pp. 64–7.
27 *RAS*, pp. 29, 224.
28 *RAS*, p. 264.
29 *CWS*, p. 204.
30 *TSA*, p. 372.
31 *TSA*, pp. 371–2.
32 See J. Gleick, *Chaos* (Heinemann, 1988).
33 D. Bohm and B. J. Hiley, *The Undivided Universe* (Routledge, 1993).
34 *SP*, pp. 28–35; *RR*, ch. 3; *SCB*, pp. 25–6.
35 *SCB*, pp. 28–9.
36 See the analysis of *GNB*, ch. 1.
37 *RR*, pp. 39–41.
38 *TSA*, chs 3 and 9.
39 *TSA*, p. 50.
40 *TSA*, pp. 152–7, 159.
41 *TSA*, p. 157.
42 *TSA*, p. 159.
43 *TSA*, p. 154.
44 *SP*, p. 28.
45 *TSA*, pp. 53–5, 158.
46 See I. Prigogine, *From Being to Becoming* (W. H. Freeman, 1980), chs 5 and 6.
47 *TSA*, pp. 59–61, 161–5, 203–6. In an interesting end note (pp. 416–17), Peacocke draws attention to three definitions of information given by John Puddefoot. None of them quite corresponds, it seems to me, to the concept of active information (cf. note 51 below).
48 *TSA*, p. 159.
49 *TSA*, pp. 54–5.
50 *TSA*, p. 164; *SP*, pp. 32–3.
51 Bohm and Hiley, *Undivided Universe*, pp. 35–8.
52 *TSA*, p. 150.
53 Barbour: *RAS*, pp. 123–4, 230–2; Peacocke: *TSA*, pp. 128–33; Polkinghorne: *SC*, pp. 48–50, 60–1; *SP*, ch. 7; *SCB*, pp. 59–61.

4 COSMIC SCOPE: CREATION

1 *SCB*, p. 73.
2 S. W. Hawking, *A Brief History of Time* (Bantam Press, 1988), p. 174; cf. *RAS*, p. 140; *TSA*, p. 134.
3 *CWS*, p. 46.
4 Peacocke: *CWS*, chs 2 and 3; *GNB*, chs 5–7.
5 Barbour: *Issues*, ch. 12; *RAS*, chs 5 and 6; Polkinghorne: *SC*, ch. 4; *SCB*, ch. 4.
6 *CWS*, pp. 79–80.
7 *SCB*, p. 75.
8 *RAS*, pp. 126–7; *CWS*, pp. 206–7; *SCB*, p. 150.
9 See P. W. Davies, *The Cosmic Blueprint* (Heinemann, 1987), ch. 14; *Mind of God*, ch. 8; cf. *TSA*, pp. 65–9; *SCB*, p. 76.
10 *TSA*, pp. 119–21.
11 Barbour: *RAS*, pp. 251–4; Peacocke: *CWS*, pp. 199–200; *TSA*, pp. 123–4; Polkinghorne: *SC*, pp. 61–5; *SCB*, pp. 79–82. Process thought sees this limitation as a matter of metaphysical necessity rather than a voluntary divine act.
12 W. H. Vanstone, *Love's Endeavour, Love's Expense* (Darton, Longman & Todd, 1977), p. 63.
13 J. Monod, *Chance and Necessity* (Collins, 1972).
14 R. Dawkins, *The Blind Watchmaker* (Longman, 1986).
15 *CWS*, pp. 105–6.
16 *IR*, p. 73; *GNB*, p. 98.
17 *RR*, p. 83.
18 Vanstone, *Love's Endeavour*, pp. 62–3.
19 *SC*, pp. 48–50, 62–4; *SP*, ch. 5; *SCB*, pp. 82–5.
20 *RAS*, p. 174; see also pp. 238–42.
21 *CWS*, pp. 199–202.
22 *TSA*, p. 68.
23 *TSA*, pp. 308–11.
24 *SCB*, p. 62.
25 *SP*, pp. 66–7.
26 *SCB*, p. 85.
27 *SP*, p. 67.
28 Barrow and Tipler, *Anthropic Cosmological Principle*; Leslie, *Universes*.
29 Leslie, *Universes*, chs 1 and 9.
30 Leslie, *Universes*, p. 204.
31 *CWS*, pp. 67–72; TSA, pp. 106–12.
32 *RAS*, pp. 135–40.
33 *SC*, chs 1 and 2; *RR*, ch. 6; *SCB*, pp. 42–6.
34 See Barrow and Tipler, *Anthropic Cosmological Principle*, ch. 1.
35 *RR*, p. 78.
36 *RR*, p. 80.
37 *SC*, ch. 2; *RR*, pp. 76–7.
38 *RR*, pp. 76–7.
39 Barbour: *RAS*, pp. 150–1; Peacocke: *TSA*, p. 345; Polkinghorne: *SC*, pp. 64–5; *SCB*, pp. 162–3.
40 See R. J. Russell, W. R. Stoeger and G. V. Coyne (eds), *Physics, Philosophy*

and Theology (Vatican Observatory, 1988), pp. 313–32; F. J. Tipler, *The Physics of Immortality* (Macmillan, 1995).

41 *RAS*, p. 151.
42 *TSA*, p. 345.
43 *SCB*, p. 165.
44 *RAS*, p. 241.
45 *RAS*, p. 241.
46 *SP*, ch. 9; *RR*, pp. 101–4; *SCB*, ch. 9.
47 *SCB*, p. 168.
48 *RR*, p. 103.
49 *TSA*, p. 344.

5 ECUMENICAL EMBRACE: WORLD FAITHS

1 See, for example, R. Hooykaas, *Religion and the Rise of Modern Science* (Scottish Academic Press, rev. edn, 1973); S. Jaki, *The Road of Science and the Ways to God* (Scottish Academic Press, 1978); C. A. Russell, *Cross Currents* (IVP, 1986).
2 Barbour: *RAS*, pp. 81–92; Peacocke: *TSA*, pp. 258–61; Polkinghorne: *SCB*, ch. 10.
3 *RAS*, p. 90.
4 *TSA*, p. 3.
5 *SCB*, pp. 176–7.
6 *SCB*, p. 191.
7 *RAS*, pp. 89–92; *SCB*, pp. 181–90.
8 *RAS*, p. 238.
9 *MMP*, p. 84.
10 *MMP*, p. 84; see also *MMP*, chs 6–8.
11 MMP, p. 144. For a contrary assessment, see K. Ward, *A Vision to Pursue* (SCM Press, 1991).
12 *RAS*, p. 91.
13 *RAS*, p. 91.
14 *MMP*, p. 176.
15 Quoted in *SCB*, p. 179.
16 *SCB*, p. 185.
17 *SCB*, pp. 185–8.
18 *SCB*, pp. 188–90.
19 See, for example, K. Cragg, *The Christ and the Faiths* (SPCK, 1986); H. Küng, *Christianity and the World Religions* (Doubleday, 1986).
20 *SCB*, p. 182.
21 Quoted in *MMP*, p. 178.
22 *SCB*, pp. 191–2.
22 See, for example, Capra, *Tao*; for critiques, see *RAS*, pp. 118–20; *CWS*, pp. 360–3; *SC*, pp. 93–4; *RR*, p. 86.
23 *SCB*, p. 182.

6 PARTICULARITY: CHRISTIAN BELIEF

1 cf. *SCB*, p. 6.
2 *SC*, p. 97.

3 *RR*, ch. 5; *SCB*, pp. 152–3.
4 *RR*, p. 62.
5 *RR*, pp. 65–7.
6 *RR*, p. 67.
7 *RR*, p. 68.
8 *SCB*, p. 153.
9 *SCB*, p. 153.
10 *TSA*, p. 94.
11 Doctrine Commission of the Church of England, *We Believe in God* (Church House Publishing, 1987).
12 *TSA*, pp. 94–8.
13 *RAS*, pp. 71–3. His most extended use of Scripture is in a discussion of human nature, *RAS*, pp. 204–9.
14 *RAS*, p. 72.
15 *RAS*, p. 73.
16 Peacocke: *TSA*, pp. 261–89; Polkinghorne: *SCB*, chs 5 and 6.
17 *TSA*, p. 262.
18 *SCB*, pp. 88, 93.
19 *TSA*, p. 262.
20 Peacocke: *TSA*, pp. 183, 268–74; Polkinghorne: *SP*, ch. 4; *SCB*, pp. 103–4.
21 *SP*, p. 46.
22 *SCB*, p. 104.
23 Barbour: *RAS*, pp. 208–14; Peacocke: *TSA*, ch. 14; Polkinghorne: *SCB*, ch. 7.
24 *RAS*, p. 210.
25 *RAS*, p. 213.
26 *RAS*, p. 211.
27 *TSA*, p. 301.
28 *TSA*, p. 302.
29 *TSA*, p. 187.
30 *SCB*, pp. 140–1.
31 *TSA*, ch. 11, especially p. 196: 'That is, in revelation God is *active*'. On the general theme of this chapter, cf. *SP*, pp. 9–10.
32 *SP*, p. 68; *SCB*, p. 137. The *locus classicus* for this understanding is J. Moltmann, *The Crucified God* (SCM Press, 1974).
33 *TSA*, p. 310.
34 *TSA*, pp. 319–36.
35 *TSA*, p. 328; cf. *SCB*, pp. 136–9.
36 *SCB*, pp. 124–9.
37 *SCB*, p. 124.
38 *SCB*, pp. 130–1.
39 *SCB*, p. 131.
40 *SCB*, pp. 135–9.
41 *SCB*, p. 139.
42 *TSA*, p. 320.
43 *TSA*, ch. 15.
44 *TSA*, p. 328.
45 *TSA*, p. 328.
46 *SCB*, p. 140.

47 *SCB*, pp. 139–43.
48 *SCB*, p. 135.
49 *SCB*, p. 139; cf. *TSA*, pp. 324–5 for a critique of this view.
50 *SCB*, p. 1.
51 *SCB*, p. 121.
52 *RAS*, p. 266.
53 *SCB*, p. 108.
54 *SCB*, pp. 66–8.
55 *TSA*, pp. 279–88.
56 *TSA*, pp. 280–1.
57 *TSA*, p. 284.
58 *SCB*, p. 115.
59 *TSA*, p. 284.
60 *TSA*, p. 283.
61 *SCB*, pp. 115–18.
62 *SCB*, pp. 108–22.
63 *SCB*, p. 114.
64 *SCB*, pp. 119–20.
65 *TSA*, p. 285.
66 *SCB*, pp. 163–4.
67 *SCB*, p. 122, a self-quotation from my *The Way the World Is* (Triangle, 1983), p. 89.
68 *SCB*, pp. 143–5.
69 *TSA*, pp. 275–9.
70 *TSA*, p. 277; cf. *SCB*, p. 144.
71 *SCB*, p. 145.

7 CONSONANCE OR ASSIMILATION?

1 Barbour: *RAS*, pp. 205–7; Peacocke: *TSA*, pp. 221–3, 321; Polkinghorne: *RR*, ch. 8.
2 *SCB*, ch. 9.
3 *SCB*, pp. 7–8.
4 H. Richard Niebuhr, *Christ and Culture* (Harper and Row, 1951).
5 H. W. Frei, *Types of Christian Theology* (Yale University Press, 1992).
6 I. G. Barbour, *Ethics in an Age of Technology* (HarperCollins, 1993), pp. 19–20.
7 Frei, *Types of Christian Theology*, p. 4.

Index

The Society for Promoting Christian Knowledge (SPCK) has as its purpose three main tasks:

- **Communicating the Christian faith in its rich diversity**
- **Helping people to understand the Christian faith and to develop their personal faith**
- **Equipping Christians for mission and ministry**

SPCK Worldwide runs a substantial grant programme to support Christian literature and communication projects in over 100 countries. Special schemes also provide books for those training for ministry in many parts of the world. All gifts to SPCK are spent wholly on these grant programmes, without deductions.

SPCK Bookshops support the life of the Christian community by making available a full range of Christian literature and other resources, and by providing support to bookstalls and book agents throughout the UK. SPCK Bookshops' mail order department meets the needs of overseas customers and those unable to have access to local bookshops.

SPCK Publishing produces Christian books and resources, covering a wide range of inspirational, pastoral, practical and academic subjects. Authors are drawn from many different Christian traditions, and publications aim to meet the needs of a wide variety of readers in the UK and throughout the world.

The Society does not necessarily endorse the individual views contained in its publications, but hopes they stimulate readers to think about and further develop their Christian faith.

For further information about the Society, please write to:
SPCK, Holy Trinity Church, Marylebone Road,
London NW1 4DU, United Kingdom.
Telephone: 0171 387 5282